101

Ways To Make a Professional Impact

ELERI SAMPSON

KOGAN PAGE

Acknowledgements

Sincere thanks go to my clients, colleagues and business acquaintances who allowed me to talk to them endlessly about 'the world of work' and for permission to quote from their experiences.

My Special thanks to my family and friends for their interest and support and very special thanks to my partner Alan Felton.

First published in 1996
Reprinted in 1997

Apart from any fair dealing for the purposes of research or private study, or criticism or review, as permitted under the Copyright, Designs and Patents Act, 1988, this publication may only be reproduced, stored or transmitted, in any form or by any means, with the prior permission in writing of the publishers, or in the case of reprographic reproduction in accordance with the terms of licences issued by the Copyright Licensing Agency. Enquiries concerning reproduction outside those terms should be sent to the publishers at the undermentioned address:

Kogan Page Limited
120 Pentonville Road
London N1 9JN

© Eleri Sampson, 1996

The right of Eleri Sampson to be identified as author of this work has been asserted by her in accordance with the Copyright, Designs and Patents Act 1988.

British Library Cataloguing in Publication Data

A CIP record for this book is available from the British Library.

ISBN 0 7494 1824 9

Typeset by Saxon Graphics Ltd, Derby
Printed and bound in Great Britain by Clays Ltd, St Ives plc

Contents

Introduction   **7**

How does this book work?   *9*

Impression Management   **11**

  1 Create the impression   *11*
  2 Look the business   *13*
  3 Project a professional image   *15*
  4 Get smart: your business wardrobe   *17*
  5 Grooming: the art of self-maintenance   *19*
  6 Brush up your people-reading skills   *20*
  7 Monitor what you say   *21*
  8 Organise yourself   *22*
  9 Monitor the effect of your personal style   *23*
10 Manage your day   *24*
11 Be assertive   *27*

Face-to-face   **28**
12 Plan to be the best person for the job   *28*
13 Make an entrance at an interview   *30*
14 Learn from others' mistakes   *31*
15 Plan to hire the best person for the job   *33*
16 Build a reputation as a skilled interviewer   *34*
17 Use the interview as a marketing exercise   *36*
18 Be a welcome addition   *36*
19 Enable the rookie to hit the ground running   *37*
20 Secure value for money and quality   *38*
21 Be firm but fair: corrections and reprimands   *39*
22 When you're in the firing line, stay cool   *40*

23 Focus on your customer's problem not on your solution   40
24 Don't be a clock watcher   41
25 Update the boss   42

Make Meetings Meaningful – Formal Groups   **43**

26 Take the minutes   43
27 Take the Chair   44
28 Chair a selection panel   45
29 Chair a meeting of volunteers   47
30 Put committees on your career agenda   47
31 Become a member of a professional institution   48

Informal Groups   **50**

32 Be a facilitator   50
33 Be an effective team meeting leader   51
34 Be a good team player   52
35 Make a team presentation   53
36 Don't be a 'human parcel'   54
37 Run a memorable training session   55
38 Build rapport   56
39 Enhance your reputation: organise a seminar   56
40 Promote yourself   58
41 Don't overdo the advertising   59
42 Know when your core specialism has become unattractive   60

Meeting The Public   **61**

43 Speak well: make a good business presentation   61
44 Avoid presenter failure   62
45 Make friends with the technology   65
46 Use your visual impact to enhance your presentation   66
47 Deal with your nerves   67
48 Introduce yourself   69
49 Say thank you   70

CONTENTS

50 Chair a conference   71
51 Speak at a conference   72
52 Be an active participant at a conference   73
53 Organise a conference   74
54 Take the applause   75
55 Keep up the good work   77
56 If you have good news, share it   78
57 If you have bad news, be sensitive   78
58 Be an expert witness   79

Going Out and About   **80**

59 Make business travel a pleasure   80
60 Keep your professional image intact when   82
     travelling
61 Look after your personal security when   83
     travelling
62 Put a knot in your handkerchief   85
63 Work, rest and play   86
64 Look after foreign visitors   87
65 When abroad: learn the culture   88
66 When abroad: speak the language   89
67 Be an effective networker   90
68 At a staff 'do' : do the done thing when you are   91
     the guest
69 Organise the perfect party   93
70 Be an ambassador for your organisation at social   94
     events
71 Be prepared to attend in-house ceremonies   95

Business-to-Business Communication   **96**

72 The telephone: know the techniques   96
73 Be an effective telephone listener   97
74 Recognise the barriers to effective listening   98
75 Use the answerphone as a butler   99
76 Transmit facts faster: fax your message   100
77 Use the mobile: choose your moment   100
78 Make the right connections: join the Internet   100

79 Use your business card as a symbol of rank and recognition   101

80 Project quality: your CV is an example of your work   102

81 Use your CV as an effective marketing tool   103

82 Write a strong covering letter   104

83 Application forms   107

84 Write a report that gets read   107

85 Get into print   109

86 Be a proficient pen-pusher: develop your writing skills   110

87 Keep a career portfolio   112

88 Keep a cuttings and clippings file   113

89 Keep in the frame with a good photo   113

90 Keep a Victory Log   113

91 Use your design portfolio as your passport to see people   114

92 Save backs of envelopes: the best ideas need a business plan   115

Press, People and Politics   **116**

93 Check for sound: using radio   116

94 Lights and camera: using TV, video and video conferencing   118

95 Understand the press agenda   120

96 Make friends with the local press   120

97 Die-stamp your mark as a professional   121

98 Become a politician   122

99 Observe the rules of business etiquette   122

100 Snap up the right training and support   123

101 Make the best of rumour, sensation and scandal   125

Further Reading from Kogan Page   **127**

Introduction

This little book will cost you less than a pizza and a cappuccino and a great deal less than a personal development course. It will do you more good and the effects will last longer. Over the years I have helped hundreds, if not thousands, of people to present themselves at their professional best. This book shares some of that experience and shows you 101 'Ways' to make an impact without resorting to stunts. Reading it shouldn't take you more than an hour or so. If you were travelling from Euston to Rugby you could read it on the way there, and on the way back make some notes on how to make the ideas work for you. There is no substitute for practice. Just reading this book is not enough. You have to try out the ideas. Personalise them and make them real for you.

Who is this book written for?

Anyone who wants to find ways of promoting themselves ethically, who is job-seeking for the first time, returning from a career break, a graduate, someone who is looking for promotion or has just taken up a new post. There are also aspects that will be useful to people setting up in business on their own in a world where appearances matter more than one might think.

What is professional impact?

It is the effect we create through our dress, voice, body language and behaviour, which in turn create our interpersonal style, our image and public face. It is also the way our idea of self, our goals and ambitions, personal values and preoccupations are communicated and received by the world. When seeking to make a professional impact, there is absolutely no substitute for sound knowledge and sure skills. However, untold damage is done to a carefully built reputation or an emerging career through a poor image or unconsidered behaviour. The ability to adopt an appropriate public persona, to look the part, speak well on your feet and handle all kinds of business situations with confidence and credibility, is a hallmark of professionalism. The advantages of these qualities are immense because people believe what they see, not what they're told. Giving other people confidence in you as a person makes them feel more secure that you can in fact do the job. Make it easy for them to believe in you and they will put fewer obstacles in your path to professional success.

Historically, there were only four professions: the church, the law, the army and medicine. There are now many more occupations such as teaching, accountancy, and architecture that we would term as professions which inform our idea of professional behaviour. In essence they are:

- a set of ethical and performance standards;
- a guarantee of competence;
- a discrete body of knowledge;
- extensive training.

Why do you need professional impact?

Because:

- Many well-qualified and able people continue to go unrecognised and unrewarded because they put themselves and their ideas across badly.
- Even intelligent and well-educated people might make little or no attempt to smooth the occasionally bumpy path of business life by paying attention to business etiquette, corporate culture and office politics.
- The power of personal style is underestimated. The importance of first impressions and the impact created by personal image inside and outside the organisation is not fully appreciated.
- Effective interpersonal, influencing and negotiating

skills are becoming more important in organisations where the corporate style encourages interdisciplinary co-operation and working in project teams.

● It is no longer possible to plan a career as a series of logical, upward steps. Two serious recessions, flatter organisations and redundancies on a large scale mean there are no guarantees of a job for life so other techniques are needed in order to get noticed.

How does the book work?

It is organised in eight chapters, each devoted to a different group of common business situations.

Each chapter illustrates how to create or lose impact. Practical advice, suggestions and anecdotes are included from experienced, successful and respected clients, colleagues and business acquaintances.

Plus 'Quotes' from the professionals past and present.

'There are many quotations in this book. I have no qualms about being a burglar of other people's words, since they benefit from further recognition and display.'

Michael Shea, *Personal Impact. The Art of Good Communication*, 1993

Plus TOP TIPS at the end of each section.

TOP TIP

Read the book from start to finish if that's your style or just browse through it. When you come across a relevant point, stop, make a note and promise yourself you will do something about it.

Impression management

Way 1 Create the impression

It takes less than three minutes to put someone off for life. Learning to manage the impression you make is a skill worth learning early on in business life. It is not about attempting to come over well in order to disguise real or perceived faults, it is more to do with the conscious management of appearance and behaviour so that the outer self is in order and ready to meet the world. The world of work is crammed with opportunities to make a professional impact. Colleagues, customers, suppliers, the boss, at a job interview, the media, new clients, new customers every day are all your audience.

First impressions

Daily business life as well as your career path will be smoothed if you consider how you impact on other people and avoid the hard work trying to undo the effects of an unfortunate first impression. Although intellectually we like to think that we are not seduced by packaging or advertising, preferring to believe that we are persuaded by rational, objective judgement of a product, service or person, research shows that 90 per cent of us make decisions about each other within a few minutes of meeting. Humans are visually dominant animals so we are impressed by what we see. Appearance counts for over 50 per cent of personal impact – race, age, sex, height, weight, colouring, body language, clothes and grooming all make a contribution. The voice and how we speak represents 38 per cent and the message or content only 7 per cent.

Suitability, reliability, attractiveness, financial status and social standing – judgements about these attributes are based on a combination of 'gut feeling' and objective observation. Sometimes it's right. Sometimes it's wrong. If you don't bother to manage the impression you create you run the risk of being misunderstood. And all this before you've even opened your mouth!

We live in what has been described as a 30-second culture. We are bombarded with persuasive images on TV, video, Sunday supplements and glossy magazines, which has made us all expert image analysts. People will judge us on the way we dress, the way we speak, the way we order our environment and the way we interact with colleagues whether we wish them to or not.

Image and visibility
Performing tasks and carrying out responsibilities only carries about 10 per cent of your professional impact. The remainder lies in image and visibility. This is why appearances do count, particularly in first impressions. This is why you should manage every moment of a first meeting and also be aware of the way you impact on other people all the time. Impression management does of course take two and there is no guarantee that your audience will respond in the way that you hope for.

The language of clothes
When we meet and before we begin to talk to each other we have already spoken in an ancient and universal language whose vocabulary consists of clothes and accessories and all forms of personal decoration. A branch of semiology, the science of signs, the language of clothes is made up of signs and symbols.

Clothing signs with a single meaning are easily read. For example, the dress of social sub-sets such as Hell's Angels is carefully chosen to reflect that group's rejection of Establishment values.

Clothing symbols are more difficult to read because they reflect an individual's personal or social agenda and can have more than one meaning. This leaves the message open to misunderstanding. Does a T-shirt printed with the slogan 'Don't ask me' mean that the wearer has an attitude problem, that they liked the way the yellow letters formed a pattern on the black background or that it was the cleanest thing they could find on the floor that morning?

Inside story

> 'I was given an excellent piece of advice by a previous boss concerning being late for work – "If a crisis occurs," he said, "whether it's emotional, physical or just a hangover, never be a bit late; always be very late. Otherwise you run the risk of tearing into the office with nerves a-jangle and everything about you signalling that something is wrong. If you take the time to compose yourself and make sure you look the part, you are half way to a business-like impression which will compensate for being late."'

Isobel Jensen, Human Resource Consultant

TOP TIP

Chameleons – people who blend in easily with the crowd – are more likely to progress in their career than Mavericks – loners who insist on being themselves.

From research by Kilduff and Day, Pennsylvania State University

---

Way 2 Look the business

Dress is one way of getting people to take you seriously. The notion of looking the part must tally with the job you do and the company you work for. Correct business dress is covered in detail in my book *The Image Factor*. The understanding of 'correct' will vary from company to company depending on the type of business, its product or service, its location, its history and traditions and so on. Historically, our idea of correct business dress comes from the male-dominated, upper middle class occupations of finance, law, medicine and the military and spread to other aspects of trade and commerce. Originally worn by men and copied by women, the modern adaptation of the post-industrial revolution Victorian model is accepted and understood almost everywhere as a uniform for business. The traditional 'Establishment' business uniform presents a formal, conservative image and can be worn by men and women. Women can interpret this model more freely than men. It consists of:

- a dark suit in navy or grey worn with white or light linen;
- small doses of colour in the shirt, tie, blouse or scarf;
- not much in the way of pattern and texture;
- dark shoes, dark hose;
- discreet jewellery;
- clean lines with a minimum of decoration;
- classic rather than fashionable styling.

Some organisations discourage Establishment or traditional City dressing because it is too formal for their product or service and they prefer their staff to dress more casually. The only way to find out what is acceptable is to ask the direct question: 'Do you have a dress code here?' Or use your eyes and play detective. The well-tried trick of waiting by the lifts or by an exit and observing the image of people as they come and go tells you more than any handbook. If the organisation's image is out of focus it will not have clear guide-lines about the image of its personnel. In which case it's simply a question of judging what you think you can get away with:

- If you are senior, dress well all the time. The more senior you are the more important it is to look the part consistently.
- If you are junior, don't wear off-duty clothes that have been demoted for work. Your seniors won't get the point that they don't pay you enough, they will think you don't take the job seriously enough to invest in a proper business wardrobe.
- If you work for yourself, don't dress badly. Wear quality clothes to project an image of success.

Personal restraint and the corporate goal

Historically, business dress has been built on the notion of restraint. Ruth P Rubinstein, the author of *Dress Codes*, says that business dress was designed to represent mastery over one's feelings. She puts it this way: 'There is a widely held belief that any legitimate business person would restrain self-expression and personal goals in favour of the corporate goal and social role.' If women want to join this game they had better get the kit and, Rubenstein again: 'minimise the maternal, nurturing and sexual dimensions of their appearance.' Dress codes are being broken down all the time. Organisations that nurture creativity and innovation often have relaxed dress codes. Others, suffering the backlash of a low understanding of casual wear are encouraging their staff to return to a recognisable business uniform.

TOP TIP

'It's the way you carry it off that's most important – it's a question of attitude – you have to be comfortable with your clothes, physically comfortable and at ease with yourself.'

Guy Speranza, fashion consultant, Selfridges

Way 3 Project a professional image

Consider your own appearance at this very moment. What immediate reactions would it provoke in the following people:

- a person of the same age and sex;
- a person of the opposite age and sex;
- a parent or one of their friends;
- a pensioner;
- a foreigner;
- a prospective employer?

We all have an image, whether we deliberately set out to design it or not. Just because you haven't consciously designed your image, doesn't mean it doesn't exist in the eyes of others. It follows that what we choose to wear for work should be carefully considered, not an accident. The important thing to remember is that clothes are a means of communication and we want to make sure that people understand the message we send out.

A professional image will:

- Do nothing to distract from your professional impact.
- In no way compromise your relationship with clients or colleagues.
- Project your company's image.
- Be compatible with the company's product or service.
- Be in harmony with your personality.
- Be consistent.
- Reflect your status.
- Convey your competence.
- Acknowledge the expectations of your clients, customers or colleagues.

Image dissonance – a hairstylist with badly cut hair.
Image congruency – a beauty consultant with flawless make-up.

A word about power dressing. It is best left to police officers, commissionaires and those ladies in leather who leave their business cards in telephone boxes. Real power is about controlling your business wardrobe so that you always have the right thing to wear.

TOP TIP

'The efficient use of a mere mirror is the first step towards communication success; the video retains the image for longer.'

Michael O'Shea, former press secretary to HM the Queen

Way 4 Get smart: your business wardrobe

Dressing well is not a gift from God. If you are not naturally good with clothes, book in to see an image consultant and buy in some expert advice. Time, money and effort have to be invested in maintaining your image through your business wardrobe. Even if you resent it bitterly – invest in your wardrobe – you are investing in your future.

The suit option for women

In a working environment where men usually wear a formal business suit, the safe bet for women is still a tailored skirt suit. A capsule wardrobe of three jackets, three skirts and eight blouses/tops based on matched and co-ordinated items will give you something different to wear every day for a month. Trouser suits look good but are risky in a very conservative firm. It is the blouses, shirts and accessories that give a different look to the basic outfits, which present the option of appearing formal, friendly, businesslike, glamorous or whatever is appropriate for the occasion.

The jacket option for women

This look is appropriate in most working environments except a very formal, traditional one. The key to a successful jacket wardrobe is to choose a selection of jackets that give you a variety of looks to match different job functions. Jackets can be worn over plain dresses or skirts and tops which needn't vary much in style or colour. A dark formal jacket worn with a matching dark skirt is the most serious look.

Accessories for women

Scarves, belts and jewellery can be classic or flamboyant according to your taste. Tights or stockings are vital to complete the formal suit option. Select from light or dark neutrals to tone with skirts or shoes. Umbrella, briefcase, watch, diary and notebooks should be in keeping with the total look, in dark colours and classic styles for a formal look, or more fashionable or eccentric otherwise.

The suit option for men

The essential wardrobe in a formal working environment, for example in banking, the law, or at senior management level, is the traditional City suit. It is also useful for client meetings, interviews and presentations. Have at least three suits on the go in medium to dark neutral colours, plain, slightly textured or discreetly patterned, six shirts that go with all the suits and as many ties as you like. (See Way 2.)

The jacket option for men

Essential items for an environment that is not too formal, for example the caring professions, will include at least three jackets and three pairs of trousers, eight shirts including two or three formal ones and a suit for the most formal occasion. Cheap shirts look worse than a cheap suit. Good quality shirts are easy to care for and are not difficult to find. They should be your priority.

Accessories for men

A good quality leather belt that can be worn with all trousers; braces for the suits as they help the trousers to hang correctly; waistcoats if you like them and they suit you; handkerchiefs in plain white or cream cotton or coloured silks to complement ties; cuff-links, umbrella, briefcase, diary and notebook in top quality classic styles; watch: one without gimmicks looks more businesslike; pen: your own fountain pen, not the office biro.

The casual option for men and women

Some jobs, because of their nature or because of the expectations of the company, make the wearing of a business suit unnecessary or inappropriate. Working in a children's home for example, or as a video technician or sculptor or poet does not usually require a business suit. A working wardrobe of casual clothes, however, still needs to be smart and look right for the job. Scruffy won't do. A well-considered wardrobe of separates will work better than any number of tired track suits or overworked jackets or 'going out clothes' that have been demoted for work.

Remember the three As

Aesthetics: choose a business wardrobe that flatters your shape and colouring and select co-ordinating colours in fabrics and textures that harmonise with each other.

Appropriateness: remember to take into account the occasion, time, place, climate, culture and expectations of the people you will meet.

Attitude: the way you feel about yourself, the company, and the job all show up in the way you wear your clothes.

TOP TIP

'If someone should stop in the street and give you a second glance then either your clothes are too tight, too new or too fashionable.'

Beau Brummell, 19th century dandy

Way 5 Grooming: the art of self-maintenance

Poor grooming is associated with being a loser. Impeccable grooming and good taste go a long way to promote your image in any organisation. Some people have never really established a proper routine of self-maintenance. This could be a symptom of squalid student days, lack of parental role models or low self-esteem. They have a hit and miss system which more or less keeps them clean and respectable and on the road. Good grooming is a habit easily acquired if you are sufficiently motivated. You can't help it if you are constitutionally weedy but at least you can give the impression of looking after yourself. The condition of your teeth, skin, hair, nails and posture all indicate how much you value yourself. If you top and tail your look with well-cut, healthy hair and good quality shoes that are well cared for, it's amazing what you can get away with in between.

People responsible for talent spotting say that even star turns get overlooked because of image breakers. The most common turn-offs are:

- bad breath;
- careless shave;
- chipped nail varnish;
- dandruff;
- overpowering fragrance;
- poor complexion;
- strange body odour.

TOP TIP

Use a breath freshener but no perfume or after-shave for face-to-face contact. One person's scented paradise is another's fly-sprayed hell. Don't take the risk.

Way 6 Brush up your people-reading skills

Body language as a form of communication has been around for ever but as a language that can be learnt and studied, only in the last 20 years or so. The business world has well-established codes of behaviour including rules about body positioning, posture, gesture and facial expression. If you are new to business life it pays to get fluent fast and learn what is usual in a range of different business situations. A confident manner, that is not cocky, being calm not over anxious, eager or submissive will mark your personal presence.

Negatives
- Holding a folder or briefcase as a barrier with hands and arms across chest and legs crossed is a highly protective pose that also looks gauche and inelegant.
- Fixing hair, checking cuticles, picking imaginary fluff all indicate lack of confidence or boredom.
- Looking down your nose by tipping your head back and looking down the line of your nose makes you look too superior. You could do this accidentally if the vari-focal

lenses in your glasses are badly aligned.
- Touching people is to invade their space and is unprofessional.
- Lolling about is irritating.

Positives

- Hands in side pockets, legs slightly apart is a stance that means business.
- Raising your eyebrows in an 'eyebrow flash' for a second when you catch a person's eye is friendly.
- A firm, cool handshake is reassuring.
- Limiting excessive use of gestures and gesticulation looks calm and controlled.

TOP TIP

Watch a video of yourself with the sound turned off.

Way 7 Monitor what you say

It pays to consider your vocal image as an important part of your total professional image. Consider what you say and how you say it. Can people hear you, do you mumble or are asked not to shout? Street, family or club language will make a negative impact outside of those places as will swearing, off-colour jokes, sarcasm and funny voices.

TOP TIP

Avoid jargon build-up.
Avoid clichés.
Avoid platitudes.

Way 8 Organise yourself

No matter how brilliant you are, you can give a bad impression in many small ways to do with how you organise yourself and your daily activities. Unless your company is in favour of 'hot-desking' you will probably have your own desk or work station. The way you maintain this area can polish or tarnish your professional image. If you have to share a work station be scrupulous about not encroaching on someone else's space. Equally, you must make sure that you are assertive about your own right to space and access.

- Deal with your 'admin' regularly. Set time aside every day or every week to deal with your diary appointments, expenses sheets, travel logs, site visit reports, sales, and so on.

- Set aside some thinking time. Difficult to do if you feel you always have to look busy but you must build in time to reassess your priorities, consider your current workload and future plans.

- Keep a day book on your desk and log all calls in and all visitors as well as jobs to be done. Date every page. Tick off in a different coloured pen when everything has been dealt with.

- Have a bring forward file into which go your papers and anything else you need for the day. Do it the night before if you are not good in the morning.

- Keep your desk clear. It's not a home from home nor an open plan trash can. Cans of coke, furry animals and good luck mascots look naff.

- Tidy your desk at the end of every working day. Crafts people know the value of tidying their workbench, putting their tools in order and checking materials for the next day. If you work with wood, metal or fabric you will know you can't beat the feeling of a job well done and a row of familiar tools sharp, clean and ready for the next job. This tidying is a symbol of the end of the working day and gets you off to a good start in the morning.

- Have a hanging file on your desk for files you use every

day which don't contain sensitive material. It looks better than a pile which could overbalance.

- Arrange for an answerphone to take messages if you are frequently away from your desk. Let someone know where you are and how you can be contacted in an emergency.
- Take messages for colleagues but be sure they receive them. Write it down and record the name, time and nature of the message. Don't volunteer what is not the caller's business. 'Mary is down in the wine bar/in the betting shop/having her legs waxed.' Use: 'Mary is not at her desk at the moment. I'll make sure she gets your message.' Don't try to judge how important the message is or act as interpreter. Just give them the message as soon as possible after it arrives. Don't be frivolous unless you are absolutely sure you know the caller. Reputations have been dented because of misplaced humour. If you get it wrong say sorry immediately.
- Make sure your colleagues know how you wish to have messages taken for you.
- Being organised doesn't have to mean living in an operational straitjacket. It's simply another kind of discipline that differentiates between a professional and a slob.

TOP TIP

Don't promise what you can't deliver. Be kind to yourself as far as deadlines are concerned. If you have made a promise, however unimportant, make sure you deliver it. If you can be trusted in small things the big ones come easier.

Way 9 Monitor the effect of your personal style

One of the most significant reasons why people don't advance in their careers is because of the effect of their personal style on others. Personal communication style does not just cover spoken and written messages but also style of dress, attitude to colleagues, how tasks and responsibilities are handled and in general terms the way you get on with people and how you get things done.

Consider the positive and negative aspects of the following:

- Always thinking you are at fault.
- Seeing the funny side of things.
- Talking loudly.
- Worrying.
- Apologising unnecessarily.
- Being enthusiastic.
- Thinking carefully.
- Being unwilling to take risks.

A technical wizard is an asset to any organisation but if he or she is unable or unwilling to communicate their ideas in simple terms that everyone can understand then boredom devalues their contribution.

TOP TIP

Be generous. Being mean in either spirit or pocket closes doors.

Way 10 Manage your day

It doesn't matter how urgently you need more time, the supply can never be increased to meet the demand. It is easy to make an impact by being a good time-manager if you work in an organisation where the standard of self-discipline is low. By the same token you can damage your professional impact by being a hopeless time-manager in a culture that respects demonstrable control of personal and business time. Being recognised as a good time-manager means having control of your business day. Dealing with the thieves of time is essential. These brigands steal from us all in different ways according to the kind of people we work with, the organisation itself and our personality and personal habits.

Well known time-brigands

- People
— inconsiderate bosses: like the ones who are on the phone all morning, go out for a late lunch and then issue the day's tasks at four o'clock;
— incompetent staff: like the ones who cannot produce a simple batch of photocopying to your standard;
— insensitive co-workers: who use work time as social time, or who don't understand that you want to get on even if it's down time for them, or who want to cry on your shoulder.
- External factors
— meetings: where your presence is required for bureaucratic or ceremonial purposes; (See Way 27.)
— paper: a human being can only get through so much documentation in a day;
— telephone calls: just because the phone rings doesn't mean *you* have to answer it.
— socialising: mixing business and pleasure is always time-consuming. Have breakfast meetings instead of business lunches. Save lunch as a leisure activity.
— bureaucracy and interruptions.
- Internal factors: self and personality
— being disorganised: can't find things, being late, being unprepared;
— over-doing routine tasks;
— failing to delegate;
— lacking confidence: going over and over something;
— keep putting things off;
— being depressed, apathetic, disinclined;
— can't say 'no';
—worry about tasks instead of getting down to them.

How to deal with the brigands

- Establish your objectives for each task then determine the steps and time scale for each task.
- Clarify your role and responsibilities occasionally so that you are not beavering away on something your boss considers to be marginal.
- Be more assertive.
- Understand your personal disposition . If you are familiar with your personal bio-rhythms you will know what time of day is best for routine tasks or more creative activities; when you are feeling your most dynamic or optimistic and can handle tricky issues.
- Check out where your time actually goes.
- Ruthlessly put portions of time aside in realistically sized, continuous chunks to be able to think, plan or act without interruptions.
- Ask 'Is it necessary in order to progress my task?'
- Ask 'What will happen if I don't do it?'
- Ask others if there is anything you do that wastes their time.

Inside story

When I first started in business I needed to pull myself out of the academic culture I was used to where time was pretty elastic and push myself into a business attitude where time is money. One of the best ideas from this period which I still use is to do with managing time on a 'days in' and 'days out' basis.

Days in include business development days in the office where similar activities are grouped together. Making phone calls, writing proposals in the morning when concentration and creativity are high, dealing with bread and butter letters and invoices, taking phone calls in the afternoon.

Days out are made up of whole days out fee-earning and using travel time to read background material for future projects or rehearse material to be used with the client. Mixed days involve seeing clients and combine fee-earning with 'go-sees'. Mixed days are even more effective when networking meetings, visits to accountant, lawyer, bank manager are built in to them.

TOP TIP

Anything involving people is going to be time-consuming.

Way 11 Be assertive

Openly aggressive, concealed aggressive, assertive and passive styles of behaviour are learnt influencing styles not personality traits. We were not born with them therefore we can change them. We usually operate through one style with a second as our back-up style and resort to the other two on an occasional basis. Aggressive and passive behaviour both lead to an imbalance of power because there has to be a winner and a loser. An assertive style respects other people's rights but respects your own too. Behaving assertively is not always the right way to behave. Sometimes a more aggressive style is needed if you want to protect someone or something and there are occasions when it is more tactful to be passive. Being assertive means doing something for yourself and doing it in a direct and honest manner.

Three assertive things you can do now

1. Say 'no' without saying sorry.
2. Take the initiative to discuss a perennial problem with a boss or colleague rather than waiting for it to blow up again.
3. Return a piece of work if it is not up to standard.

TOP TIP

Make it clear that you are interested in personal development opportunities or specific training to upgrade your skills instead of waiting to be asked.

Face-to-face

Way 12 Plan to be the best person for the job

Why do so many of us tow the dread of interviews behind us like a trailer? We remind ourselves of miserable interviews with head teachers, of hopeless oral examinations. We imagine a hostile situation with ourselves as the passive victim harangued by fierce strangers. We picture all the nasties in the world gathered together in a strange building in an alien city, where we will encounter aggressive strangers who will ask us questions that we don't know the answer to.

The notion of dealing with the situation on equal terms seems to dissolve like sugar in tea. If this is the baggage you bring to a job interview then you deserve to suffer, particularly if part of the pain is caused by not allowing enough time to think, plan and prepare your strategy and rehearse your performance. Your image and reputation are at stake whether you are selected or not. So it pays to think positive and get on with the rehearsal. Being short-listed means someone already thinks you could do the job. You will have been invited in:

- to see if you 'fit';
- to test your confidence and show you are not crushed by nerves;
- to establish how convincingly you can sell yourself – to observe the degree of control you have over yourself and your material in an artificial situation.

Why do candidates still turn up for interview without doing their preparation? The answer is probably a combination of factors including not knowing what kind of research to do or how to go about it and not being able to see the need. A business-like letter confirming the arrangements for the interview is a good start.

1. Prepare

Write down a simple sentence that states the purpose of the interview. Keep reminding yourself what it is. Prepare statements about yourself, your beliefs, your experience and your suitability for the post. State the facts simply without boasting. Recall anecdotes and evidence that back up your statements. Practise sentences that begin: 'I have a reputation for being . . .', 'My colleagues tell me that . . .'

2. Plan

Decide what you want to get out of the interview. Plan time for preparation and research. Build it into your schedule. Plan the interview day itself so that you are not rushed or with half a mind on something else. Plan your travel arrangements.

3. Research

Take up any opportunities that are offered to visit the organisation or to have an informal discussion about the post. Find out about the organisation, its reputation and financial status, who will be interviewing you, check how long the interview will last, where and when. Find out about travel arrangements, reimbursements for overnight accommodation, train or taxi fares. If part of the interview is going to include making a short presentation then check availability of audio-visual facilities.

4. Rehearse

Rehearse your lines to anyone who is willing to act as an audience: friends, family, the cat. Time your answers. There is no need to go over one and a half minutes except for the most complex of answers. If you speak at the average rate of 120 words per minute then you have 180 words available, which is plenty of time for a clear concise response. Practise getting to the heart of your message in 30 seconds. Rehearse stories, examples and anecdotes that bring your experience alive. Don't exaggerate or underplay your successes. Be honest about your failures but be prepared to say clearly what you have learnt from them. Don't over-rehearse. Just make yourself thoroughly familiar with your material so that you feel comfortable with it and can sound spontaneous.

The interview is the show-case for your skills and talents. Don't waste it.

'It's amazing how many people prepare themselves to fail the interview. . . thinking of all the reasons why they should not get the job. We call these "wooden legs". Popular wooden legs are:

I will not get the job because:
  —I am too old/young
  —I am not/too qualified
  —I am not/too experienced
  —I've spent too much/too little time in my present job'

The Perfect Interview by Max Eggert

TOP TIP

The worst sins of a candidate are: waffling, long-windedness, showing off and liking the sound of their own voice.

Way 13 Make an entrance at an interview

Working on the principle of the effects of primacy and recency our audience is going to recall the impression we made at the moment of arrival and have a lasting picture of our retreat. Actors work hard to make their exits and entrances on cue and to make them memorable.

Be yourself but make sure it's your best professional self. If your self-awareness is low on these matters then find out about yourself. Do some research. Ask a friend or colleague how you look and how you behave when you feel nervous, when you are relaxed, when you feel shy or get bored. Use video recordings of family or training events as reference.

Don't freeze up
It really is all right to show enthusiasm, energy, and animation; to move, to gesticulate, to change your position. Rigidity, a flat face and no hand gestures convey a lack of connection to the event, fear, or not being in control. No opera singer, rock star, or after-dinner speaker would dream of making an entrance or an exit without a rehearsal. Not just one, but many. They will decide how to walk, where to stand, what gestures to use. The effect is assessed for vision,

sound and charismatic appeal by a team of people whose job it is to check it all out. We don't have that team but we do have cam-corders and honest friends. We should not be afraid to use them.

Don't forget your exit
When it's time to go, make a proper exit. Don't sit down and squash your best line. Don't stand up as you speak. There is more impact if you stand up first then give your exit line.

TOP TIP

Practise the following sequence on entering the inter-view room (or restaurant, or office).
Head up – breathe out – shoulders down – enter – pause – sweep the room with your eyes – make eye contact – smile – shake hands – speak – sit down.

Way 14 Learn from others' mistakes

The following advice to other candidates always comes up during a debriefing session but not necessarily in this order:

1. Arrive early.
2. Take all the paperwork with you in a folder which also contains a pen. You won't need a briefcase or a handbag.
3. Know your material, especially your CV, after all you are the expert. A natural familiarity with the material works better than a glib or over-rehearsed response. Be prepared to answer probing questions:

   'What was the reason behind your move from British Consolidated to UK Metals?'

   'What would you like to be doing in five years' time? What skills, qualities, experience and beliefs do you have that will help you to realise this goal?'

   'Most young managers are going down the MBA route. You aren't. Why not?'
4. Have an opinion. If you haven't got one draw a parallel with something on which you do hold an opinion.

5. Be aware of current 'hot issues' in your specialism or pro-
    fession, in your own industry and in business generally.
    Read the paper that morning.

    'In twenty years time there will certainly be a cure for
    cancer. How will this affect your industry sector, the
    pharmaceutical industry, the cancer charities?'

6. Listen carefully. Be ready to pick up on comments and
    special words or phrases used by the interviewer. Flatter
    them by playing back what you've heard.

7. Watch for the boredom factor. Stop talking immediately
    the interviewer looks bored.

8. Never underestimate the power of non-verbal behaviour.
    Use eye contact. A genuine smile shows confidence.
    Offer to shake hands. A firm, not bone-crunching, hand-
    shake is an asset for men and women. Have a cotton
    hanky in your pocket to discreetly wipe a sweaty palm
    (don't use paper tissues, they disintegrate).

9. Don't argue with the interviewer.

10. Take some trouble with the interview outfit. It usually
    goes down well if it looks as though you have made an
    effort to acknowledge the occasion. Female candidates
    have a more precarious line to tread because women
    analyse other women more shrewdly.

The best interview outfit will:

- be comfortable;
- be practical;
- be flattering;
- reflect your personality;
- support your professional message;
- give you confidence;
- conform to the company's team strip.

TOP TIP

Dress to impress, not to kill.

Way 15 Plan to hire the best person for the job

M J Yate, writing in 1988 in *Hiring the Best,* succinctly described what constitutes the 'right' appointment. 'A person who is able and willing to do the work, someone with team spirit and who is manageable, a professional who fits the corporate image and who is personally compatible with your company's place on the corporate evolutionary scale. And of course an emotionally mature adult with sound and rational judgement.'

Even if you are not a human resources specialist you could be asked to interview for a new member of the team. As a newcomer to interviewing the number one question is – how do you go about recognising the right person for the job? The answer lies in describing the job they will have to do as clearly as you can and drawing up a job description and person specification that will attract the right kind of candidate. Give careful scrutiny to the CVs and covering letters that result and investigate any other background material that might help. As a new interviewer, I often had to check up on qualifications I'd never heard of. You can't skimp on preparation otherwise you will be sucked into a morass of prejudice, false impressions and expediency.

Find your own style as an interviewer

Have a plan, then personalise it. For example here is a classic plan for a one-to-one interview that could be adapted to your own style:

1. Start and finish in a friendly but business-like manner. Be sure to use a comfortable and natural way to establish rapport.
2. Outline the interview, its timing, purpose and structure.
3. Talk through the CV
   — education: reasons for choosing A levels, choice of university, any prizes, awards, scholarships;
   — professional: qualifications: how achieved, full time, part time, home study, timescale, any re-takes;
   — experience: what kind of organisations, reasons for

joining/leaving, main areas of responsibilities, key achievements, any difficulties, any gaps.

4. Sensitive and probing questions to find out about candidate's aims and ambitions, their way of thinking, some indication of the intra-personal – their motivation, personal anchors, set of professional values and beliefs.

5. Behavioural questions based on specific job related criteria: 'What would you do if . . .' You need to set up the situation so that you get an idea of the full range of their capabilities.

6. Off the wall questions if it has all been a bit dull.

7. Close the interview expressing the hope that the candidate has had an abundant opportunity to present themselves favourably.

8. Thank the candidate for coming and let them know what will happen next and the time scale of events. Make sure the candidate leaves with their self-esteem intact even if yours is a bit shaky.

Suppose the candidate fits the whole specification? Do you cheer? No: if there is no room for them to grow into the job, they'll do the job, get bored and sooner rather than later – push off!

Open your mind
A closed mind or years of tradition could blind you to seeing just the right person when they present themselves to you in flesh or on paper.

TOP TIP
Good questions usually get good answers.

Way 16 Build a reputation as a skilled interviewer

Candidates will gossip. Aggressive, bored or under-prepared interviewers get talked about. If you are new to interviewing you need to build your reputation as a skilled and fair interviewer.

Take notes
Record the evidence as you hear it but it is kinder not to make a note just after the candidate has fluffed a reply or made a mistake.

Feedback
It is polite to give feedback to unsuccessful candidates if they ask for it. Honest advice will be much appreciated by the unsuccessful candidate and, if carefully delivered, will enhance your professional image and reputation as an interviewer.

Tissue rejection
Never underestimate the importance of 'fit'. Carelessness in the selection process may cause a high turnover rate in a team or department. Personal style that is not in tune with the organisation's style may produce 'tissue rejection'. In medical terms, when the host organism spots an intruder it rejects it.

Inside story
There was once an accountant with a local council who was responsible for selecting an assistant to head up a new finance project. It was an internal appointment so he and the panel knew all the applicants. Having drawn up a short-list, they decided that in order to get the best person for the job they would be scrupulously fair and not take into account any prior knowledge of the candidates. They would make the decision based solely on the candidate's performance on the day. As it happens, the candidate with the best qualifications and experience was also universally disliked. She did an excellent interview and was appointed.

Result – disaster! Within a week she had got up everyone's nose and had to be moved to another project on the same salary and the panel had to start all over again.

TOP TIP
Remember the legal framework. For example, your notes could be subpoenaed if there was a tribunal.

Way 17 Use the interview as a marketing exercise

The interview is an ideal sales platform and a wonderful opportunity for the interviewer and their company or department to present themselves as favourably as possible. A candidate should leave with a positive impression feeling that they had a fair hearing and treated with respect. Stress interviews should only be required for stressful jobs.

TOP TIP

Be mindful of cultural pitfalls. No interviewer can hope to be aware of all the subtleties of cultural differences in a multi-racial society. A skilled and fair interviewer will make sure they are not influenced by the differences.

Way 18 Be a welcome addition

For the first few days in a new job you feel vulnerable and exposed just like going to a new school. You try to fit in and not be a nuisance. You attempt to get the practical stuff about names and places and positions of things sorted out and then settle down and hope someone will give you some real work to do. (See Way 19.)

Make a good impression by turning up on time, being appropriately dressed, look keen, smile and show an interest in everything.

TOP TIP

Have a notebook with you all the time so that you can note down instructions, key names, numbers and other pieces of information so that you don't have to keep going back to check up.

Way 19 Enable the rookie to hit the ground running

The aim of an induction process for an individual or a group of new recruits such as a crop of graduates should be to make sure that the new recruit has a good start and hits the ground running. The most successful method is the one that strikes a balance between company objectives and the pressing concerns of the newcomer. The first few days will leave the newcomer with information overload anyway so, offer help in bite-sized pieces. Reinforce important information regularly, either verbally, on a message pad or via an E-Mail system. A nice touch would be to make sure the newcomer has a lunch date every day for the first week. Find some real work for them to do such as background reading, looking for information in a report, analysing data, making telephone calls.

Put yourself in their shoes. Ask yourself what you most wanted to know when you first arrived at work. A checklist might include:

- Toilets.
- Canteen.
- Telephone systems.
- Local customs, for example 'dress down Friday'; working through lunch with sandwiches at the desk.
- No personal or incoming calls.
- Usual hours worked, whether everyone usually gets in early or stays late or goes to the pub.
- Security locks, code numbers, identity tags.

Some companies issue all new staff with personal organisers with a page of this kind of information, which is very thoughtful. Anxiety is a very strong barrier to retaining new information.

I worked for a short while for a security-conscious firm of accountants. I found the ladies room easily enough through the swing doors in an adjoining corridor but didn't know you needed a swipe card to get back into the training suite. After 20 minutes the waitress laying the table for directors' lunches spotted a nearly hysterical me through the glass door, took pity on me and let me in.

TOP TIP

Introduce the newcomer with their full name and mention one of their assets: 'This is John Napier. He is taking over from Phil and has the international experience we've been looking for.'

Way 20 Secure value for money and quality

The Concise Oxford Dictionary defines the word *appraise* to mean: to estimate the value or quality of, or to set a price on, by an official valuer. No wonder boss and subordinate alike feel uncomfortable with the experience, particularly if it is linked to a possible rise in salary. People being appraised don't like being judged like cattle in a ring. The person in the role of valuer can be nervous about their ability to do the task and about the possibility of their observations going on record. Some of these difficulties can be sorted by appropriate training and open communication. It is never possible for either party to be wholly objective but it is possible to set up an atmosphere where:

- praise can be given;
- future targets and objectives can be discussed;
- failings can be acknowledged. . . by *both* sides.

Inside story

In my first year at art school the drawing tutor was puzzled by the notion of appraising the students' first-term work. He insisted that the quality of our learning could not be measured by ticking boxes on a form and that anything of value would be in our heads ready to use in the future. He decided that a measurement of quantity would be as good as an estimate of quality and so the next morning he brought in a pair of scales and solemnly each of us stepped forward to have our portfolios weighed.

TOP TIP

Any kind of feedback about your performance is like being given a bag of Pic'N'Mix. Say thank you whether you think you will enjoy the contents or not and sort through it later and find your favourite.

Way 21 Be firm but fair: corrections and reprimands

Problem employees drag down morale, spoil the company image and distract you from more important tasks.
Perennial discipline problems include:

- Attitude problems: complaining, pessimism, lack of enthusiasm, energy or commitment.
- Skills problems: out of date, never had the skills, lack of training, lack of judgement.
- Misguided: work hard but not at what you want, make mistakes, don't share your priorities.

Your professional image as well as the company's image will suffer if you don't sort them out. Because of a strong need to be liked there is a resistance to saying unpleasant things. You know you can't be loved by all of the people all of the time so presenting a professional image by being firm but fair will attract respect. Calm and control are the key words.

TOP TIP

'I encourage my staff to respect two rules with regard to disciplinary meetings:
1. Disagreement is not disloyalty.
2. Remember the MBF rule: Manage By Fact.'

Polly Sampson, document centre manager, Rank Xerox Business Services

---

Way 22 When you're in the firing line, stay cool

A disciplinary meeting is no place for high emotion. If you find yourself called to a disciplinary meeting make sure you understand *why* you are there. Gather all the facts and consider why you did what you did. Was it carelessness, wilfulness, sabotage? Was there really something else bothering you? Use this opportunity to present your case.

Ask for training, support or supervision. If a follow-up meeting has been promised make sure it happens. Carefully consider any recommendations and the implications for your future in the company and what it might mean in terms of a reference if you should go for another job.

If an apology is in order, give one.

'Poverty and shame shall be to him who refuseth instruction: but he that regardeth reproof shall be honoured.'

Proverbs chap.13: 18

TOP TIP

Have a 'buddy' present for a serious matter. Their role is to act as a witness and see fair play. Your 'buddy' could be your line manager, union representative or family member.

Way 23 Focus on your customer's problem not on your solution

Everyone is in sales. They sell in two parallel ways all the time:
1. As a representative of their company whether they are in the sales department or not, selling to the rest of the business community.
2. As a representative for their own ideas, point of view, professional opinion or specialist information, selling to internal or external clients.

Powerful professional impact rests with being able to focus on your customer, find out what they need and give it to them rather than push what you have to sell.

'Selling often attracts good lovers: people who are smart, con-fident, and at ease with other people. But selling is more than just good conversation and a relaxed manner.'

Seductive Selling by Kit Sadgrove

TOP TIP

Take the time and effort to prepare for a sales pitch as if for a date with someone special.

Way 24 Don't be a clock watcher

Find a balance between being married to the job and knock-ing off on the dot. Always leaving tasks half-finished to rush off to catch a particular train appears unprofessional. If the way things are organised at work is really in discord with your lifestyle maybe you need to be a little more assertive about your needs. Challenge the need for five o'clock meet-ings if you have children to meet from school and the meet-ings could be held earlier in the day.

If working hours are 9–5 then you have to check out local custom and practice, whether it means getting in early enough to be ready to start work at nine or whether it really means arriving at nine and starting work at some point after that.

Inside story

For a very short while I was based at County Hall, the Headquarters of the late Inner Education London Authority. Used to being a freelancer, I was amazed by the clock-watch-ing, a common aspect of process culture. I was used to an environment where you worked until the project was com-pleted. It wasn't my way to stop everything even in mid-sen-tence the minute the hands of the clock ticked round to clos-ing time. What I found even more amazing was that work stopped ten minutes before going home time to allow for a visit to the ladies to freshen up, to say goodnight to friends in adjoining offices and to wait for the lifts which could be a little temperamental so that one's body was seen leaving the building on the stroke of five.

I could only presume my work mates didn't love their jobs as I did. My colleagues presumed I had an unhappy home life. Another lesson I learnt was that I could never be happy working for a Government department.

TOP TIP

Be brave enough to go home early if you finish something ahead of schedule, particularly if you have a young family or domestic commitments. Be sure to let the right people know you've finished the job.

Way 25 Update the boss

Send your superiors frequent progress reports. Keep them informed of targets met, difficulties solved, tasks completed. Choose an appropriate style; a memo, an E-mail message or an informal verbal report when leaning in the doorway. If you are experiencing difficulties, be part of the solution not part of the problem.

TOP TIP

Have three ideas ready to offer and let your boss choose one. This will work better for you than just dumping the problem on them and hoping they will solve it for you.

Make Meetings Meaningful –
Formal Groups

Way 26 Take the minutes

Don't flinch if you are asked to take the minutes at a business or professional meeting. It's another opportunity to make yourself known and doesn't have to be a chore. Make it easy for yourself by making a plan of who's who and who is sitting where. No one really expects verbatim minutes (if they do, then use a tape recorder and get the proceedings transcribed) but they do expect a correct record of decisions taken and everyone wants credit for their ideas. Work as a team with the Chair. To do this job well you need to be a naturally good note-taker and have a dispassionate view of the proceedings.

Touche Ross *meeting notes*

△

Client	Prepared by:	Date:
	Reviewed by:	Date:
Purpose of meeting		Date:

Attendees:

Type of meeting (incl. telephone conversations):

Minutes of meeting/Action points   Action

                                        Who   When

An example of a meeting planner

The author wishes to thank Touche Ross for their kind permission to use the above.

TOP TIP

'Colour code the paperwork, be consistent – we use pink for minutes and green for the agenda and bright yellow for anything that needs to grab attention. It's also useful to have a committee handbook or terms of reference available at every meeting.'

Suzanne Davison, administrator

Way 27 Take the chair

In some companies you can never get hold of anyone when you phone in. They are either at a meeting or on a course. Seventy per cent of a manager's typical day is spent at meetings. One-third of these are probably unproductive. Most of us would agree on what makes an ideal meeting so why don't we do something about it? Because, however appalling they are, many meetings are comforting and familiar, like junk food. One route to the ideal meeting is to take the Chair yourself. If you are new to chairing or have got into bad habits you may like to consider the following:

1. Don't meet unless you have to. Would a memo or a message do just as well? Abandon the 'Monday morning meeting' if there is nothing to discuss.

2. Limit numbers to eight or fewer. Get rid of the non-contributors. People who are only there because they have to be will contribute aggravation and distractions, like a disruptive child in class.

3. Have a clear purpose. Communicate that purpose to all those present.

4. State the start and finish time. If extra time is needed to reach a decision on an important point, negotiate with *all* the participants for time needed to complete the business. If you can't get agreement, don't go into extra time.

5. Have a timed agenda. Balance long and short items, put them in order of priority. Wear your watch on the inside of your wrist. You can glance at discreetly or make a play of it whichever needs to be done.

6. Do not allow tabled papers. All papers should be submitted in advance to allow sufficient time for people to read and digest. Long papers or those containing a mass of data or detail should be accompanied by a short précis. Let your committee know why the papers are being sent and what opinion or decision or action will be needed from them.

7. Be exceptionally well prepared. Read everything that comes in. Talk to people between meetings. Build bridges. Collect evidence and information. Show by example that you expect the same standard of preparation from everyone else.

8. Encourage participation. Make sure you use people's names to include them in the discussion. Don't allow silence.

9. Eliminate 'Any Other Business'. If the atrium's collapsed, the company's gone bust or the finance director has eloped with the window cleaner, everyone will know about it anyway. AOB is used an excuse to introduce controversial business and get it past on the nod when everyone is tired.

10. If the meeting has to be cancelled of course you would let everyone know but station someone at the venue anyway to apologise and explain to anyone who didn't receive the message.

TOP TIP

Do not allow any 'action replay'. If anyone was not at a previous meeting or wants to go over an issue one more time, be firm – don't let them. Line up a patsy for dealing with awkward customers on the committee. Use 'Chairman's Action' as a last resort.

Way 28 Chair a selection panel

Look as though you have authority, give the lead and inspire confidence in both the candidate and the panel members. Poor chairing skills will let the situation get out of control, the panel may run out of time, there could be unfair or illegal questioning, the candidate might feel intimidated or that they have not had a fair hearing. This is all bad news for your professional image. Here is a well-tried plan for a 40-minute three-member panel interview:

Topic	Time	Who
• Rapport, icebreaker	2	Chair
• Introductions	2	Chair
• Warm-up questions	5	Panel (1)
• CV questions	7	Panel (2)
• Technical/professional questions —1 main and/or 2 or 3 follow up	7	Panel (1)
• Thought process/problem solving questions —1 main and/or 2 or 3 follow up	7	Panel (2)
• The 'vision' question	3	Panel (1)
• Why us	2	Chair
• Why you	2	Panel (2)
• Any questions	2	Chair
• What next, thank you	1	Chair

Experienced interviewers are never under-prepared and their real strength is that they've seen and heard it all before. They know how to get past the camouflage to what is underneath.

TOP TIP

'Re-read *everything. Make notes highlighting pertinent issues and relevant questions. Know your panel and know how to use them. If the interview has lost its dynamic or you feel you are not getting behind the person, shake it up a bit and ask an unexpected question. For example:"It has been said that those who can, act, and those who can't become agents. How does this apply to the way you would approach this job?"'*

Jennifer Bowden, managing consultant, Human Resource Solutions

---

Way 29 Chair a meeting of volunteers

Personal politics can be a thug even in the most genteel of organisations. Whether we are talking about a Residents' Association, The Gas Consumers Council or the firm's ski club, making an impact as the chair of a group of volunteers involves the combination of chairing skills and the ability to meld disparate souls and their personal politics into a working team. Don't allow in-fighting.

All volunteers need to know what they can bring to the party, so be prepared for a lot of auxiliary work out of the meetings. As Chair you need to know what motivates each of the members and to make sure that their time, skills and talents are well used. It is most important to see that they are thanked privately and publicly for their contribution.

'It is essential for the Cabinet to move on, leaving in its wake a trail of clear, crisp, uncompromising decisions. That is what government is about. And the challenge to democracy is to get it done quickly.'

Clement Attlee

TOP TIP

A committee usually likes to feel that they belong to a special group and that their Chair is the one with style and charisma. Feed this notion.

Way 30 Put committees on your career agenda

This 10-point plan applies to all meetings, particularly those where you do not have a clearly defined role but need to project professionalism, confidence and competence.

1. Arrive early. Enter confidently.
2. Sit in a visible position from where you can catch the eye of the Chair. Take up your natural space. Sit relaxed but alert and open.

3. Make sure you speak early on.

4. Make your key points in clear, concise terms. Be direct.

5. Make one sentence per point.

6. Offer up your opinion. Don't keep it to yourself or else why are you there? Intellectualise, generalise, globalise – save the detail for working parties.

7. Use a firm tone of voice, lower the pitch but turn up the volume control if necessary.

8. Hitch your comments to someone else's remarks or report if you fear that yours on their own won't have enough weight.

9. Know when it is right to make an impact – when to fit in, when to stand out.

10. Leave promptly. Don't hang about unless you want to use the opportunity to network or canvass someone. If you are managing your time properly you should have somewhere else to go or someone else to see.

TOP TIP

Test your level of insecurity. When invited to attend a meeting ask yourself what would happen if you didn't go. If you must go, make sure you are fulfilling part of your career agenda:

- To learn something – news, views, gossip you couldn't pick up any other way.
- To promote yourself.
- To impress someone.
- To increase your visibility.

Way 31 Become a member of a professional institution

Membership of a professional body looks impressive on headed notepaper but it is also a measure of your competence and commitment. Membership offers opportunities for networking, exchange of ideas and socialising. These are common benefits of membership but many professional institutions have tight entry standards and are in no way a cosy club. Membership through an evaluation of your experience plus peer group vetting can in some ways gain more respect than examinations. It suggests that you really can do the job and not just write papers about it. Membership of one or more professional institutions is an indication of professional credibility, and if nothing else in a competitive market is useful in getting a place on a short-list.

If you have to attend meetings set yourself some ground rules. Be clear to yourself about why you are there, your role and remit. What can you contribute? State and re-state it to the meeting if necessary. Find out the expectations surrounding the role and the history of it. If you are there as a representative, avoid giving only the party line. If people can predict what you have to say then why waste their time? You might just as well construct a cardboard cut-out of yourself holding a banner printed with the party line. Prop it up in your usual chair and then go shopping

---

TOP TIP

Avoid getting on your hobby-horse. It's so boring and other people just switch off.

Informal Groups

Way 32 Be a facilitator

The role of a facilitator is not unlike that of a Chair but has some special characteristics that make it significantly different. A facilitator is there to serve the group in order to make their objective more easily achieved. This is done by enabling and encouraging all members of the group to feel equal, to feel able to contribute and to make all participants feel valued. They must make sure that there is meaning and purpose to the gathering.

Throughout the meeting a facilitator will check that the physical environment is right and that time-scales are being met. The role requires maturity and an ability to be silent when necessary and speak up when necessary; to listen very carefully and follow the flow of the debate as well as the undercurrent of feelings and emotions. All of this without dominating, leading or taking decisions for the group.

Management consultants Carole Tietjen and Peter Walker use the analogy of growing something from seed:

FACILITATION

The seeds –
the agenda
The pot –
the setting or environment in which the meeting takes place
The compost –
the fertile medium of all the minds at the meeting
The germination –
the discussion and growing of lots of ideas
The potting on –
appraising the ideas and selecting the strongest
The flowering –
the agreement and acceptable product

TOP TIP

A good facilitator helps to make things happen but is not a manipulator.

Way 33 Be an effective team meeting leader

Making your mark in a gradeless organisation that operates with flatter structures means project work, sometimes as a team leader and sometimes as a team member. Leading a team means that your professional credibility is at stake internally as well as with clients. In modern companies there are more teams about and they come in many guises:

- self-managed work teams;
- project teams;
- problem solving teams;
- creative teams;
- management teams.

The role of the team meeting leader is to motivate the team towards a common goal. If you find yourself in the role of team leader with the responsibility of chairing team meetings, the following guide-lines should help if the role is new to you:

1. Make sure everyone contributes. No sulks or silences.
2. Ask for specific ideas, don't allow rambles round the topic.
3. Be open-minded or you might miss the best idea.
4. Don't get flustered or angry.
5. Stay positive, use positive language.
6. Allow time for discussion and reflection but keep the team focused on the project
7. Evaluate progress. Identify weak and strong areas.
8. Reinforce good work. Make sure everyone understands which areas need improvement and agree an improvement plan.

9. Notice the contributions of your team members and who takes on which kind of role. Some people take on several roles, others stick to one or two. Observe who you've got and how they operate.

When you know how the team inter-relates you can use its combined force more effectively. Understand the Push-Pull factor.

TOP TIP

Be generous. If as the project leader you earn a lot more than the team, even temporarily, treat them for a job well done. Paying for a meal out for everyone, funding an evening's Go-Karting or a day at a health farm is imaginative and generous and will enhance your reputation more than by just providing a round of drinks after work.

Way 34 Be a good team member

As the traditional organisational pyramid breaks down, more staff will be involved in the daily process of decision-making. Being a good team member means being independent sometimes, taking responsibility for your particular tasks and delivering to the team to standard and on time. Take an active part in team briefings and be aware of the role you and others play.

Which of these do you do?
- Praise others.
- Maintain harmony.
- Resolve conflict.
- Look after hurt feelings.
- Resist change.
- Keep the team optimistic and positive.
- Manage the team's use of time.
- Manage the details.

- Urge the team to produce results.
- Make lists, take notes.
- Sell ideas.
- Suggest ways to move on and change.

TOP TIP

Take your natural role because that will be your strength but be prepared to flex your role when the situation needs it.

Way 35 Make a team presentation

The whole team may sometimes be asked to present its work. It could be to an external client or to an internal management team. The image and professional credibility of the team needs to remain intact. It pays to agree to set aside planning and preparation time for the project. The team must meet in advance to agree the main points and the house style they will use in terms of language and visuals as well agree individual roles and responsibilities. A run-through is vital otherwise it's going to look uncoordinated and amateurish. Agree a running order and then decide on what props or equipment to use. Decide who will speak, when. Agree the topics and the supporting materials.

Choose an unofficial chairman who will keep order and see that questions are passed to the best person to answer them. Each member of the team must be responsible for their own preparation. Don't argue or disagree with each other in front of your audience. Each member should only answer questions on their specialism as agreed in advance. Show supportive body language to whoever is speaking. Don't show irritation, exasperation or disagreement. Sort it out later.

Look like a team by deciding in advance what to wear. You don't have to resort to a uniform but it is effective if you can agree on a degree of uniformity in clothing that underlines the team spirit but emphasises the differences in personality, message or expertise – for example, the same style jacket in different colours; a specially designed project tie for men or scarf for women; everybody agrees to wear navy.

TOP TIP

Use the team name or project code on all support material, slides, OHP acetates and documentation to reinforce the team's identity.

Way 36 Don't be a 'human parcel'

Making an impact at a seminar or training session means wanting to be there in the first place and not being 'sent'; being willing to learn and being prepared to make a contribution by being an attentive listener; asking questions and making observations. Irrelevant remarks, disruptive behaviour or waffly questions make you appear foolish, are boring for the rest of the group and irritate the presenter. Think positive. Turn up on time and dress for business unless you are invited to dress down. Look interested even if you're not, you may learn something or meet someone interesting.

Waffle. Long, complicated statements, particularly if they are off the point, really put people off. Someone using the occasion to climb on to their old hobby-horse is a real turn-off and won't get listened to.

Wrong agenda. I have heard people bend a discussion about art displays in the foyer to problems with personal security on the campus car park. A serious problem, of course, but on the wrong agenda and likely to turn off prospective supporters.

Your reputation is better served by saying how your point is relevant to the discussion, making your point briefly, indicating whether you agree or disagree with the presenter, then being quiet. If you've aroused some interest then anyone who wants to take it up with you can do so.

> **TOP TIP**
>
> *'An ideal delegate is someone whose manager has worked with them to identify their training needs accurately. They will understand why they are receiving training and what is required of them. Most of all they must want to learn.'*
>
> Gatwick Airport Ltd

Way 37 Run a memorable training session

Many people who are not professional trainers are at times asked to run an informal training session for colleagues around their specialist subject, or about the implementation of new regulations or systems, or may be asked to give an update on the legal implications of a current business scenario.

Make it interactive

Everything we know about adult learning suggests that *learning by doing* is the only way. All participants in a training session must be actively engaged during the session or else they will be bored by the material and fail to apply what has been presented to them. Use different learning approaches. Games, simulations, questionnaires, quizzes, discussion groups, case studies, video. Don't skimp on time for introductions, ice-breakers and rapport-building. (See Way 38.)

Have a lean curriculum

Only include essential elements. It is useful to find out any previous knowledge and build on that. A pre-course assignment will help to establish levels of interest and ability. A colleague phones up one in eight of the delegates and chats to them in advance about what they *need* to know and builds the course outline round that information. If you want people to concentrate on the activities of the day, provide written support material for them to take away.

TOP TIP

We learn with all our senses. So why not reinforce new material with smell, taste or touch as well as sound and pictures.

Way 38 Build rapport

Most professional presenters would agree that the success of their work depends on their ability to build rapport with the group within minutes. Similarly, someone who finds themselves in the role of unofficial trainer needs to make the right impression quickly.

Getting on to first name terms quickly and making sure that everyone knows and uses each other's names can settle people down quickly. A small repertoire of games and exercises that can help people to get accustomed to using each other's names will avoid a common communication barrier which can be created by unusual names. A reliable device is to encourage your audience to make a connection from the unknown to the known. I was grateful to a delegate on a course who helped us all by saying 'My name is Goura, you say it like Laura with a G.'

TOP TIP

'Rapport – don't leave home without it!'

Máire Brankin, Oxford Executive Coaching.

Way 39 Enhance your reputation: organise a seminar

A seminar can be defined as a small group with a common interest assembled for discussion or research, but who may or may not all be specialists in the subject. A seminar doesn't only have to take place at a university.

Advice for the débutante seminar leader must include this from *How to Give an Effective Seminar* by Watson, Pardo and Tomovic:

1. Create a topic.
2. Gather material.
3. Prepare the seminar.
4. Deliver the seminar.
5. Initiate group discussion.
6. Encourage feedback.

A dissertation or thesis written for an academic or practical course of study, an MBA for example, makes an appropriate topic. An elegant and professional way of saying thank you to people who have been helpful, a seminar demonstrates that you have not been away on a 'jolly' and also gives the organisation a chance to demonstrate their support for personal and professional development. Organise an enjoyable event with a food and drink element. The invitation list should include:

- Your boss: maybe your boss would like to act as Chair or even host the proceedings.
- Your professor: ask him or her to say a few words about the course you attended and the significance of your dissertation.
- Anyone from the organisation who has been particularly supportive.
- The person who was responsible for funding your study.
- Friends and family. This is an excellent opportunity to show them what all the fuss has been about.
- Someone from a specialist, technical or professional journal who could write up a favourable report or who could commission you to write a piece for them.

Prepare an abstract of the paper in simple language and make sure everyone who attends has a copy. Make sure you include your name, address and telephone number. Include thanks and acknowledgements where appropriate. People who don't like a fuss in public still appreciate being thanked.

Plan and prepare for the event with extra care, then relax and enjoy and use the occasion to sell yourself as well as your topic. *Pay for the event yourself if necessary*. It will be worth every penny in terms of visibility and goodwill.

TOP TIP

Be prepared for ill will from colleagues who did not think of the idea for themselves, who are jealous of your success, or who did not take advantage of the opportunities you had.

Way 40 Promote yourself

I went to the kind of school that encouraged modesty, frugality and being a good loser. I realised that I was culturally biased against the idea of business and was in all ways unprepared to run my own. A disinclination for mentioning money and a feeling that my talents should speak for themselves were disadvantages to be overcome. Enthusiasm overcame modesty and the discovery that there is nothing dishonourable about making a profit made me structure a clear scale of fees.

No promotion – no sales
No sales – no profit

To make your mark in an organisation or as a freelance, you need to market yourself and make yourself visible. If everyone in an organisation works hard then image and visibility become more of an issue. One of the reasons why extremely able people fail to make their mark in a job is because they do not promote themselves or worse, give the wrong impression. People can be overlooked for an important project or assignment simply because they have not registered their interest in it. They come across as disorganised or apathetic, when to themselves they are just being low-key or modest.

Deal with low visibility

Every organisation and every business sector has what Rein, Kotler and Stoller* call its 'constellation of high visibles'. Everyone in the trade knows them and respects them but they are unknown outside their sector. If your job has low visibility you need some VGM – Visibility Generating Machinery. Keep on the look-out for opportunities to promote yourself, your ideas and your values:

- Get used to the idea of publishing your work. This means through reports with your name on, writing letters, features, articles or books.
- Socialise a bit more. Let people see you around.
- Be an active networker. Use your contacts inside and outside the organisation. (See Way 67.)
- Join up. Join appropriate professional associations and support groups and *go to the meetings*. (See Way 31.)
- Know the system. In any organisation there is always a system. To get yourself noticed you have to acknowledge the system, learn how it works and how to work the system.

'If I want to knock a story off the front page', Hillary Clinton reportedly told her aides, 'I just change my hairstyle.'

TOP TIP

The best talent could be in your own organisation. Train people to promote themselves.

Way 41 Don't overdo the advertising

Overt displays of personal advertising are a real turn-off. Don't pull a series of publicity stunts. Let your achievements spread by word of mouth. Get to know the influencers professionally, don't accost them at a social level.

---

* *High Visibility – The Professional Guide to Celebrity Marketing* by Irving J Rein, Philip Kotler and Martin R Kotler.

TOP TIP

Superior results are gained by letting other people act as your publicity agent.

Way 42 Know when your core specialism has become unattractive

Nothing makes you look more stupid than not knowing what you should have known. 'I haven't had time to read the report yet. I didn't know they'd taken that drug off the list. I didn't know the code had been changed.' Equally stupid is producing goods or services that no one wants.

Credibility and being currently knowledgeable are both important elements of professional impact. Your credibility is your insurance policy. Keep up the payments by making sure you know what's going on in your immediate specialism, the one you are paid for. Keep up to date. Make absolutely sure that what you are doing is needed by your company or your industry sector. Read the business pages, use your networks.

TOP TIP

Develop an instinct for knowing when your core specialism has become unattractive and it's time to fine-tune it, change it or move on.

Meeting the Public

Way 43 Speak well: make a good business presentation

Most people would rather have a tooth pulled than speak in public. Fears usually fall under one of three headings:

1. Looking a fool.
2. Feeling a failure.
3. Forgetting what you wanted to say.

Many a good case has been lost through poor presentation. This is not an argument for promoting style over content, it is simply echoing the wealth of academic research that says the *how* of presentation is more influential than the *what*. The ability to communicate well at all levels is increasingly important because people are used to being on the receiving end of polished presentations at conferences, in the media and elsewhere. You must be able to make competent business presentations and present your case well or your credibility and therefore your professional image will suffer. You can't just read about this one. You have to do it and learn from your mistakes. There is no reason why you should not present yourself well and with confidence. There are courses run in-house in most organisations but if you can't get on one or there isn't one, then you must find a public course and fund it yourself.

Content
Revise your script and use more 'yous' than 'Is'. This will make it more audience-centred and in an instant make it more interesting.

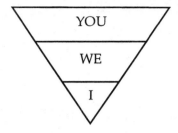

Voice
Inject some energy and feeling into your voice. Practise by singing along to a passionate song.

Dress
You are still your best visual aid.

Body language
Shoulders down, feet slightly apart. Have a home base at centre front that you can return to if you tend to wander about the platform. Make eye contact with the audience by sweeping the room with your eyes in an 'M' or 'W' pattern.

TOP TIP

'Sing – like you don't need the money.
Dance – like there's nobody watching.
Love – like you'll never get hurt.
It's got to come from the heart if you want it to work.'

Country and Western song

Way 44 Avoid presenter failure

The most common presenter problem is failure to create a relationship with the audience. This is closely followed by over-concern with detail, then by over-confidence and under-rehearsal. Many people in business have to make occasional presentations, which are usually short but critical to their careers. It might be a ten-minute presentation at a selection interview for instance, or a short presentation at a board meeting or staff conference, or maybe a vital report to a client. Seasoned and inexperienced presenters alike can talk too much, drown in the minutiae of their material, or allow themselves to become a slave to technology.

Presentation plan

The following formula has proved successful in helping people to sort out their ideas, their objectives and an appropriate style of delivery. After checking that the content can't be faulted shift the emphasis to structure and delivery so that the presentation is more relevant and more interesting.

This is a sure-fire plan for a ten-minute presentation that can be adapted to suit any time allocation. The plan shows that there is only one minute for each point so it pays to rehearse getting to the heart of your message in 30 seconds (approximately 50–60 words) supported by an illustration in a further 30–60 seconds.

Another feature of the plan is that each point should be illustrated in a slightly different way by making reference to a current news item for example, or including some historical background or local colour, facts and figures, a cartoon, or asking the audience a question. A genuine attempt to reach the different personalities and preferences in the audience is always well received. Focusing on the start and finish, on your entrance and exit, is another feature of this plan. Elegant, amusing or punchy, the impact you create will rest with the opening and closing of your presentation, so these two elements need the most preparation.

The presentation plan can be drawn up and put on to a single A4 or even A5 sheet and laminated or put into a plastic folder (traditional cue cards are too small for this system). An example is shown over the page.

SUBJECT:			
Topic	*Time in minutes*	*Body Language*	*Props*
Entrance and opening remarks	½		
Introduction	1½		
Topic A point 1	1		
point 2	1		
Topic B point 1	1		
point 2	1		
Topic C point 1	1		
point 2	1		
Summary	1½		
Exit and punch line	½		
Total	**10 minutes**		

If you already have plenty of material this is a way to concentrate on making your message clear and your presentation memorable. This plan is an excellent discipline and always works. It has been used by scores of my clients. To guarantee success, time must be put aside for ruthless editing and for researching appropriate anecdotes and evidence and most important of all – *rehearsal!* There is no substitute for experience; we all have to learn how to do it by doing it.

TOP TIP

Change some aspect of your presentation every 30 seconds or so. Smile, move forward, ask a rhetorical question, pause, whisper, slow down or speed up the pace.

Way 45 Make friends with the technology

Being a successful communicator means that you remove as many barriers as you can between you and your audience. This includes the technological barriers.

- **Lectern** – should have a light, clock and control panel.
- **Microphone** – pinned to your lapel or neckline; a wandering mike gives you freedom to roam.
- **OHP** – maximum six line message in large letters.
- **35mm slide projector** – excellent for pre-prepared presentations that go round the country with you.
- **Slides** – many software packages are available which will help you to produce visually interesting, top quality slides.
- **Laser pen** – use to point to the screen.
- **Infra red remote control** – hand held, not taped to the lectern, gives you freedom to move about.
- **Audio** – useful to allow the audience to listen to sounds other than your voice.
- **Auto cue and Video script** – your script can be relayed via a monitor for your eyes only.

All good presenters learn to work from a visible watch or a clock.

> '*Once the game plan is sorted out, the next serious stumbling block is using technology that limits rather than liberates – the single biggest culprit being the lectern, the fixed block to which the presenter becomes shackled for the entire presentation . . . All that is needed to remove these restrictive shackles is an infra-red remote control for the slide changer and a lapel microphone. You then have the freedom to move around and to prove to the audience that it's not a cardboard cut-out doing the presentation.*'

Tony Miller, Training Director, Frizzell Insurance, in *Financial Training Review*

Inside story
A new chief executive appointed a script-writer for his first

shareholders' meeting. They didn't get on and argued every word and phrase. On the big day his speech went on to autocue as planned. It went very well to begin with then the autocue rolled round: 'You're on your own you pompous b. . .'

TOP TIP

Move away from the lectern. Use it as your base position to hold your notes and props but don't speak from it unless the occasion is very formal, you are very tall and you are a powerful wordsmith.

Way 46 Use your visual impact to enhance your presentation

1. Always stand up to present at a formal event.
2. Wear a jacket, keep it buttoned up. A well-defined shoulder line looks more impressive. Avoid fussy detailing at the neck area. You want the audience to focus on your face.
3. Avoid distractions from your main message by wearing anything too short, too tight or too transparent, or anything that is likely to come adrift.
4. Glasses – get a non-reflective coating on the lenses. Avoid wearing tinted or photochromatic lenses indoors, they look a bit sinister.
5. Choose colour carefully. A small audience will be overpowered by strong bright colours, so select a colour scheme from the navies, greys and beiges lifted with some colour near the face in the form of shirt, tie, blouse or scarf. A large audience can take a more dramatic look using stronger colours. Dark colours are more serious.
6. Choose your style carefully. Who in the audience do you need to impress? The more radical your presentation, the more conservative your clothing needs to be.

7. Check your background. Will you merge into it or stand out? If the background is dreadful, position yourself in front of a flip chart or white screen.

8. For women – If you have to join a panel on the platform check that there is a modesty cloth covering the table down to the floor – lack of one is entertaining for the audience, embarrassing for the presenter.

9. For men – Remove pens, loose change and keys from pockets. This reduces temptation to fiddle and they spoil the line of the outfit anyway.

10. If presentations affect you physically – make you fidgety, pace about, get sweaty – then make sure you have a comfortable, familiar outfit that gives you room to move and absorbs sweat. A fresh cotton blouse or shirt is a good starting point. Rehearse the whole outfit before the day. Pay special attention to grooming. Looking good makes you feel good and you will convey this to your audience who will then respond positively to your presentation.

TOP TIP

Dress up a bit more than your audience expect – they'll love it.

Way 47 Deal with your nerves

If you're not nervous you're not normal. When you are nervous adrenalin flows through your system. The trick is to use the rush of adrenalin to work for you, not against you. Nerves are not a nuisance, they are the mechanism by which your body prepares you for the big event.

If you don't know what you're talking about you deserve to be petrified. If you haven't prepared properly there is no quick fix. If being unprepared makes you nervous build in design and planning time as well as time to collect material. Average presenters may get away with less than thorough preparation, star performers, even household names, never break the rule about thorough preparation and rehearsal.

Stay in control
- Say 'no' if the request to present is unreasonable because you are not the right person to do the job or not enough time has been allowed. Everyone's reputation will suffer if you make a mess of it.
- Don't drink. Alcohol gives a false sense of security.
- Get some air into your lungs by steady breathing. Big deep breaths might make you faint.
- If tension builds up in the neck and shoulder area, drop your head slowly forward on to your chest and gently roll in a half circle.
- If your mouth dries up bite the tip of your tongue to make the saliva flow.
- Think of your audience not yourself, try positive visualisation, enjoy the experience. Think of the good to your reputation when it goes well.

Pray for something to go wrong
What is the worst thing that can happen? Get your worst fears out in the open and talk about them. Store up ways you can prepare yourself to deal with them. The truth is you need things to go wrong so that you learn how you behave under pressure and store up the experience to make you stronger another time. You need to know what it's like to face up to and have succeeded with:

- a hostile audience;
- difficult questions;
- your mind going blank;
- breaking wind;
- equipment failure.

TOP TIP
You don't have to be perfect to be successful.

Way 48 Introduce yourself

Be clear about the purpose of the introduction at the beginning of a presentation or seminar. Unless all your personal data appears in the programme, the audience would like the facts stated for them – who you are, why you are there, what your credentials are and to confirm the topic and your angle. The person making the introductions should state the rules about timing, questions and interruptions, do their best to set the right tone for the proceedings and build up a pleasant air of anticipation.

Introduce yourself if you don't trust your hosts to do it properly, or write your own introduction for them to use. In order to evaluate not only your own performance but how it has been topped and tailed, the micro-cassette is a valuable friend. I recorded this and kept it as a good example of someone using my material and moulding it to their style:

> *'What do BT, NHS managers and the staff at our local library have in common? They have all benefited from the expertise and enthusiasm of our next speaker this evening. Considered to be an expert on the language of clothes she's just come back from advising a hospital board on the selection of new uniforms for community nurses. She is going to talk to us tonight about non-verbal communication. Let me introduce Eleri Sampson from Positive Images.'*

If they are competent they will use your information even more effectively. If they are not very good then at least they should get the facts correct. A clear, factually correct introduction sets the appropriate tone for the talk to come. Unlike this example also captured by the micro-cassette:

> *'Can everyone hear me? OK. Now then who have we got? Oh yes, tonight's speaker is Hilary Simpson. She's one of our little local businesses. [I run my own business with a local office and a nation-wide client base.] If I'd known it was you Hilary, I would have smartened up a bit (snort and giggle). I haven't heard her speak myself but she's supposed to be quite good. I expect you'd like to tell us about yourself Hilary and give us some idea what you'll be covering tonight. Over to you then.'*

Use introductions to promote yourself and introduce your-self in terms of what you want from the meeting, what your values are or what you want to do next in career terms rather than mention your company or your job title. It'll help you to make your mark but doesn't sound pushy if you rehearse it so that it sounds natural.

Inside story

When I was at teacher training college there were two lectur-ers with the name John Brown. The first John Brown came on to the stage in the lecture theatre and said 'Good morn-ing. My name is John Brown – I teach sociology and I'm the one who always wears a red rose in his buttonhole.' We never forgot him.

TOP TIP

People don't always understand what you do or what your job title means, so why not practise a few 30-sec-ond 'signature tunes' to play to people when you meet them for the first time.

Way 49 Say thank you

Saying and writing thank you is almost a forgotten art. Reviving it could be a shrewd move to increase your impact socially and professionally. We all know how it feels when we receive genuine thanks, even if we were only doing our job. 'Thank you for your help in making the parents' evening so successful.' 'Thank you for the basket of flowers you sent while I was in hospital.' 'Thank you for releasing the funding to allow me to attend the course last week. It was a valuable two days. I was able to meet some useful contacts from other companies and learnt some valuable techniques that will be put to work straight away. I would not hesitate to recommend it to other senior managers.'

TOP TIP

Make an impact with a short, sincere, handwritten note, a card if you feel unable to write more than a couple of words, or a telephone call within 24 hours.

Way 50 Chair a conference

How can you use this very high profile opportunity to build your professional reputation? If you are invited to take this role do you know what it is likely to entail? Attending a conference yourself will give you an idea of good and bad chairing styles. What is certain is that you will have to concentrate all the time, even when you are not speaking. You can't take your eye off the ball for a minute. All the rules of good chairing apply (see Way 27) plus a few more. Learn from other Chairs and develop your own style.

- Set the tone of the occasion through your choice of dress, style of behaviour and vocabulary.
- When you introduce and thank the speakers, do it gracefully and naturally *and don't steal their thunder.*
- Control the timing. Go with the mood of the occasion. If a speaker is going down really well let them have a little longer if they need it and then adjust the timetable. If a speaker is making a hash of it or going on too long you must use an assertive way to get them off.
- Control questions. If the sound system is not good or the questioner has lost their way it is a kindness to repeat the question for the benefit of the rest of the audience.
- Be prepared to deal with hecklers and cope with the press.

TOP TIP

'You can't be too well briefed. Think through the whole thing first and make sure you are briefed on everything – the main purpose of the gathering, who is speaking, who will be in the audience and who to contact if anything goes wrong. Travel up the night before if necessary.'

Caroline Langridge, Head, NHS Women's Unit

Way 51 Speak at a conference

Speaking at a conference or even at a fringe event is very good visibility. Preparation is everything. The rules of effective presentation apply (see Way 44) but the occasion could be more formal than you are expecting and the audience could be in hundreds, if not thousands.

Delivery
Whatever you do, *don't read your script!*

Unusual illustrations
All subjects benefit from illustration and example, particularly academic, scientific or technical subjects. Many of us rely on words and ignore the other senses. A speaker at a Health Services Conference in the Midlands endeared himself to the audience and made a memorable point about human resources and the need for selecting the right people to fit the job by showing us a brightly coloured child's toy. It wasn't only the parents in the audience who recognised the pertinent choice of the hollow ball which had a variety of different shaped holes through which you tried to post matching shapes.

Focus
At a management conference an imaginative but low-key speaker started his first session by lighting a candle and waiting for the whole room to focus on the candle and quieten down before he started. It takes courage and patience and a strong presence to get away with this but I have seen many variations of the focus technique work well, particularly with a group of participants who do not know each other.

Record of the event
Sometimes you will be asked for your permission to have audio or video recording made of your presentation. This is further exposure if the tapes are to be sold or a transcript published in a professional journal.

Ask for a minder

Someone who is delegated to meet you and look after you for the day, sort out fees and expenses, glasses of water and so on is worth gold.

> 'Good briefing makes your speakers relax so that they can show themselves at their best. Pleasure in their subject, a sense of excitement and looking happy to be there is what the audience want of a speaker.'

Mel Gibson, Youth Librarians Group Conference Secretary

TOP TIP

Arrange for someone to record or even video-tape your contribution. If it's good you can use it as part of your promotion plan. If it's not so good, congratulate yourself for having made the effort and learn all you can from the tape.

Way 52 Be an active participant at a conference

Gain some visibility and increase your reputation as an intelligent participant by asking a memorable question. If the proceedings are being recorded or will be written up later, make sure you say your name, designation and company clearly and give a short indication of the background and reason for your question. Then ask the question or make the comment in no more than 30 seconds. Study the list of attendees. Approach anyone who looks interesting or useful.

TOP TIP

Don't be shy about telling the speaker how much you learnt from their presentation and how much you enjoyed it. The warm glow it creates will spread to both of you.

Way 53 Organise a conference

A conference can be quite a small affair. It doesn't have to be on the scale of a political party annual conference at a seaside town. It could take the form of an awayday for a group of managers wanting to plan the following year's business strategy, or a learning set wanting to get together to hear about the latest developments in their special area of interest, or an annual event for a group of like-minded professionals.

Organising a successful conference will increase your reputation for months. There are opportunities for meeting, greeting and being visible. Even fielding the complaints, if you do it well, will enhance your professional image. Use a reputable venue-finding company. They can take away all the headache of researching the venue and handling the booking procedure. They should have reports of all the venues they use and may be able to get you a discounted rate as well.

In advance

- Determine the objectives of the event.
- Draw up an audience profile.
- Decide on budget.
- Decide on type of venue. A management centre can offer a more businesslike environment and state-of-the-art technical equipment. Hotels are usually good at food and service. The right place will have both.
- Consider the appropriate location.
- Visit the venue.
- Timing is important. Half-term holidays have obvious advantages and disadvantages.
- Choose the meeting room.
- First impressions will matter.
- Decide what type of catering will be needed.
- Review accommodation and find out who needs what, whether different grades of staff traditionally have different accommodation, what things should be settled on a personal account or via the corporate account.

- Meet the venue staff.
- Confirm everything in writing. Get a written reply. Keep copies. Take them with you on the day.
- Read the small print, especially anything to do with cancellation clauses.

On the day
Check layout, equipment, noise, daylight, air-conditioning, heating, external noise, obstacles, chairs, tables, AV equipment, check what is included and what will be an extra charge. Either do these things yourself or make sure that whoever is delegated to do them reports back to you.

Design a planning sheet if the venue don't provide their own

TOP TIP

'You must know your venue. Nothing can put you at more of a disadvantage as the organiser than being caught out about fire drills, relocated lavatories or restricted access.'

Combination Venues of Marlow

Way 54 Take the applause

Internal or public awards and the attendant publicity are good for business. Look out for anything suitable that you, your team or company could apply for. Even if you don't get short-listed the process of the application and the goodwill it can engender is worth the effort.

If you have been short-listed but don't know for sure if you have won, prepare a speech and plan a platform outfit anyway. Keep your speech short. Make it funny if you know you can be amusing under stress. If you don't know, don't risk it. Rely on the organisers to show you what to do, where to stand, where to go next, adjust the microphone, point you at the photographers.

If modesty is getting in the way of your accepting an

award, don't take it for yourself, accept it for the pain it will cause your competitors.

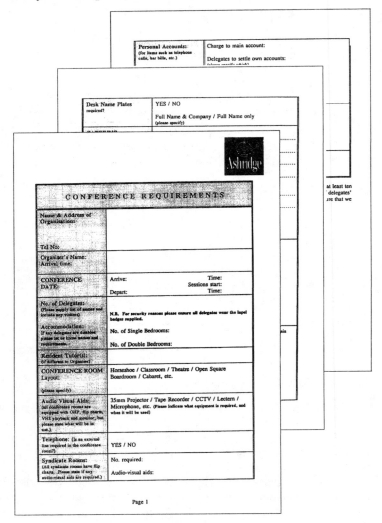

The author wishes to thank Ashridge Management College for their kind permission to use the above.

TOP TIP

If you are the recipient wear something that looks terrific but does not sabotage your entrance or exit. *Smile* – hit the target directly – say thank you – don't get emotional – get away.

Way 55 Keep up the good work

Charitable giving is a personal affair but public fund-raising for a good cause is fuelled by publicity. Business-to-business publicity through the local newspaper, radio station, in-house journal or a charity's own newsletter can spread the word about good fund-raising ideas as well as raise the profile of the individuals concerned.

> *'We started a newsletter to the business community so that people can see that there are other companies out there contributing and may see ways that they can join in themselves. We like to develop a relationship with companies and hope the first donation is like the little acorn from which the big oak tree is going to grow.'*

Shaun French, corporate development officer, Action For Kids Charitable Trust

---

TOP TIP

Get your photo with that of the recipient and a news item in a charity's business-to-business newsletter. The story should say how much you collected, how it was done, who benefited, and include thanks all round.

Way 56 If you have good news, share it

Everyone likes to hear good news. Tell anyone you think would like to know about any good news that is relevant to them: costs have gone down, profits have gone up, targets have been met, disasters avoided. This technique keeps your name in the frame and does the recipient some good too.

TOP TIP

Make a note to be the messenger with good news. When people ask you how you are the answer is always: 'Fine.' No one wants to hear your troubles unless there's gossip involved.

Way 57 If you have bad news, be sensitive

A senior medical consultant always used to say: 'There is no bad news there is just news. Let the patient decide for themselves whether it is good or bad.' The same advice applies to career news. Notice of redundancy is not so bad if you were thinking of starting up your own business, and failure to get a promotion may be welcomed if you are pregnant. Prepare to take the flak anyway. Ideally, bad news should be given face to face. It may feel uncomfortable for you but you must handle it. If it really is bad news prepare yourself to answer two key questions:

- *Why me?*
- *Why now?*

Check that the way you look and your manner support the message. News about a lost promotion won't go down any better if you are wearing your Mickey Mouse tie and wobbling cucumber joke egg-timer set to signal the end of the interview.

TOP TIP

Your image will suffer if you don't learn to deliver bad news sensitively and to pick people up afterwards.

Way 58 Be an expert witness

Always looks interesting on a CV and intrigues people at dinner parties and networking events. Credibility is all. Dress, voice, body language all working to one aim – a high believability factor.

TOP TIP

'When you are in the witness box with the might of the law all around you it is normal to be nervous. A court of law is a highly conventional place whatever the subject of the case. Remember that you are not talking to the jury, you are there to explain the technical points to the judge. Knowledge is the key thing but you must also look the part.'

Martin Shoben, director of studies, London Centre for Fashion Studies and expert witness

---

Going Out and About

Way 59 Make business travel a pleasure

Business travel has the potential to be a pleasure or a nightmare. Careful planning and intelligent research should smooth the way. If you have any problems, someone who's done it before will always have the answer. So, get on the phone. Ask. You won't look stupid, just keen. Whether you are travelling at home or abroad, for a few months or a few days, the success of your trip will depend on appropriate planning and research combined with a sense of excitement. A good place to start is with some key questions:

- **Who?**
  Make sure you always know who you are meeting. What is their job function/level of seniority/purchasing power? Is there any chance either of you might be wasting your time?

- **Why?**
  What is the purpose of the trip? Are both sides clear about the objectives? Is it strictly in order to do business or a bit of a jolly? Be honest. You can then prepare appropriately. Are you just delivering goods or services or are you expected to include some sales or PR, speak at a conference while you're there, see if you can do a bit of recruitment, or get drawn in to disciplinary proceedings.

- **Where?**
  This country or abroad? Some essential research will include finding out about:

1. The climate, weather conditions – hot, cold, humid? Sunglasses required at all times?

2. Social and business customs – handshake, kiss or bow?

3. The location. Where will you be staying? In the town or

country, a rural backwater or a cosmopolitan hotel with international standards? Maybe a cheap and cheerful B&B or the firm's Management Centre or even as someone's house guest?

- **How long for?**
  What is the length of the trip – two days, two weeks, two months? What should you take, what arrangements should you make for your absence?

- **What?**
  What is the trip made up of? Meetings? Presentations? Sightseeing? You could be sitting down all day in fierce air-conditioning clamped to a simultaneous translation head-set. Or you could be expected to attend early morning meetings and entertain yourself for the rest of the day.

- **How?**
  Contemplate your itinerary. Is the route new or familiar? Do you have to change planes or trains? Are there any complicated transfers or more than one country, more than one town? Check what you need in the way of pass-ports, visas and so on to get in and get out again.

- **When?**
  Take into account the time of year you are travelling. Are there any special local or national considerations to be aware of to do with the climate, a national holiday, market day, war!

Once you've answered these questions you will then be able to concentrate on what to wear, what to take and how to behave.

TOP TIP

Photocopy your passport so that if anything should hap-pen to the original at least you have a record of the num-ber and where and when it was issued. You could save frustrating hours or days in a consular office or embassy while a duplicate is being prepared.

Way 60 Keep your professional image intact when travelling

These wardrobe tips are useful for both men and women:

1. You never know who you might meet and anyway you get better service when you are appropriately dressed.

2. Select travel-friendly clothes that will:
   — shed creases
   — allow for expansion
   — adapt to heat and cold, formal and informal situations
   — not attract dirt
   — not retain perspiration.

   Jersey and knits, wool or cotton with lycra content, layers and elastic waists all fit the bill. Comfortable shoes are an essential.

3. Dress up rather than down. It's easier to create a more casual look from formal basics than it is to try to look smart from casual basics. Individual garments that will mix and match will give extended wearing value and will work better than carefully matched outfits that can't be interchanged.

4. Restrict your colour scheme. Conservative, neutral colours in medium to deep tones look business-like, don't show the dirt and are the most adaptable. Choose accessories from one colour family then they will go with everything. For leather accessories stick to one colour. Either black, navy, tan, dark brown or stone. For jewellery stick to gold or silver, not both. For scarves or ties limit the colour choice to one or two shades that harmonise with the main outfits.

5. Use in-house facilities for ironing, dry-cleaning and valeting. Use your energies for business not for housekeeping.

6. Travel light – don't overpack. Travelling light with one carry-on bag means your luggage goes wherever you go. Don't overpack. If you are travelling to a country about which you know very little then pack as little as possible. Stick to your usual business dress then when you arrive, see what everyone else wears. Buy what you need locally. What else are credit cards for!

TOP TIP

Women travellers. Wear a wrap rather than a coat or rain-coat. It looks more elegant and can do duty as a blanket in a cold hotel room, a pillow on a long flight, and a dressing gown in an emergency.

Way 61 Look after your personal security when travelling

The risk of something happening to you when you are travelling on company business is statistically very low. However, many people, particularly women, do not feel safe when travelling. You can ruin your professional impact by arriving somewhere important looking strained, worried or frightened. This is not just a problem for women travellers. Men and women should give some thought to how and when they travel and take some basic precautions:

- Tell people where you are going, your route and when you expect to arrive.
- Leave a contact number, take your mobile phone along or some small change and a phone card for emergencies.
- If you change your mind about anything let someone know. Carry a personal alarm.
- Always sit in the back of a cab. Don't chat about personal things. If at any time you feel uncomfortable ask the driver to stop at a busy place and get out.
- In a hotel, keep your room number to yourself and your room key concealed.
- Trust your instincts. If the situation doesn't feel right it probably isn't – so get out of it!

The Suzy Lamplugh Trust 4 Point Plan

1. Be prepared

— Prepare yourself for the journey by making sure you know your way.

— Familiarise yourself with your surroundings and be aware of escape routes.

— Be careful what you wear. Avoid making yourself an easy target.

2. Look confident

— Walk with a sense of purpose.
— Radiate non-vulnerability.
— Watch your body language.

3. Avoid risk

— Decline offers from strangers.
— Keep to familiar territory where possible.
— Avoid spur of the moment choices.
— Look out for traps.

4. Never assume

— It won't happen to me. Nobody is invincible.
— I can cope. Meeting aggression with aggression can get you hurt.
— It's only a short journey. Be prepared to go the long way round to avoid trouble.
— They look respectable. So do many murderers, rapists and pickpockets.

When meeting strangers

If you have the kind of job such as estate agent, recruitment consultant, home sales or financial adviser where meeting strangers is a regular event, it pays to be vigilant. You don't want to come across as a fusspot or a wimp but you do need to have some personal guide-lines if there is not a company code of practice in operation. The Health and Safety Act has recently been redefined to include the personal safety of employees.

1. Record the name and address and telephone number of your client in a log that can be accessed by colleagues or your family if you work from home.
2. Re-dial the number before you leave to check its authenticity.
3. Meet at your office.

4. Don't give out your home phone number or address.

5. Ask a colleague to go with you if you feel at all uneasy.

6. Have a report-in system so that you call or are called after every visit.

7. Record any difficult moments, even if you handled it well, so that a colleague is not put at risk another time.

8. Prepare a coded signal that indicates distress so that you can give the alert without compromising safety.

TOP TIP

Do everything necessary to ensure your own security and peace of mind. You can't give of your professional best if you are worried about being harassed or in danger.

Way 62 Put a knot in your handkerchief

So many venues have sophisticated facilities and complimentary products that you risk looking very insecure or eccentric if you take everything but the kitchen sink. Don't waste valuable packing space, save space for your business needs. Your laptop will be more useful than a hairdryer, which is standard in all but the most basic of venues. Valeting, room service, concierge and housekeeping are all there to be used. All you have to do is decide what you want to pay for. Phone ahead and find out what the venue offers and what their charges are.

Make up your own sewing kit for emergencies if housekeeping staff are not available. Hotel freebies won't have buttons that match your shirt or threads in colours that match your jacket, or needles with eyes large enough to thread when you are so cross you can't see the eye and your hands are shaking because you are late or hungover.

If you prefer to be self-sufficient *don't forget:*

- Swimming costume or exercise kit.
- Small safety pins and elastic bands have their uses too.
- Small roll of sellotape – very efficient way of removing dust and fluff.
- Plastic hanger to drip dry shirt or blouse.
- Travel-size stain and spot remover in a leak-proof container.
- Addresses and telephone numbers of local business contacts or friends and relations in the area in case you have time for a visit or a meal.
- Phone numbers of business base and family for keeping in touch, and emergencies.
- Also for emergencies – carry with you the name and phone number of your next-of-kin.
- Relaxing or absorbing book or magazine.
- Travel bag large enough to take everything but small enough to carry, with an external pocket for travel documents, a newspaper and umbrella.
- Personal radio/stereo/CD player.
- Herb tea bags.
- Favourite chocolate or fruit.
- Tiny travel alarm if you don't trust hotel room wake-up technology.

TOP TIP

Have a set of envelopes marked up with date/project/client/city to take receipts for expenses.

Way 63 Work, rest and play

If you travel by train, plane or chauffeured car you can choose to use this time to work. You can catch up on your reading, write up some notes on the lap-top or just have clear thinking time. If you travel first class you can build in some relaxation time. Buy in whatever you need in the way of appropriate time and space, facilities and technology, and peace and quiet in order to operate as a professional. If your company are not enlightened in this way, fund it yourself. If you want to be left alone you must develop a firm line in assertive brush-offs and closed body language.

TOP TIP

If you don't want to work when you travel you can use travelling time to rest and relax. You can either avoid human interference or actively seek it. If you would prefer some company the dining car or buffet on the Intercity 125 is very sociable.

Way 64 Look after foreign visitors

Impress foreign business visitors by researching their needs. You hope that your guests will do their own research and adapt to the local way of business but some attitudes are so deeply ingrained that they can't be changed. If you know what to expect you can prepare yourself to be tolerant and respect religious and cultural differences. Obvious differences occur in:

- **Eating and drinking habits**. New Yorkers for example are used to a huge variety of eating places. It is useful to find restaurants that serve vegetarian or kosher food.

- **Dress**. Some visiting Australians or west coast Americans are not used to wearing a suit and tie for business; it would be kind to warn them in advance what your company dress code is.

- **Business practice**. Americans, for example, like to start on time, Arabs don't see lateness as being rude, the French like to shake hands on meeting and departing.

- **Smoking**. Business people from Italy, Spain, Eastern European countries and Russia haven't yet got used to No Smoking buildings. Find somewhere to meet where having a cigarette is not going to cause a fuss.

If you find yourself responsible for looking after visitors, check whether they speak English and find out if they would like an interpreter. Prepare documents in both languages.

TOP TIP

Practise a simple 'Welcome to our company' speech in their language.

Way 65 When abroad – learn the culture

Cultural fluency is more important than language proficiency. Understanding the values and attitudes that underpin business life in other cultures is what counts. The culture, social customs and business behaviour of other countries might seem to a visitor to be quaint, romantic or even barbaric depending on their own upbringing, experience and values. We are more likely to achieve results when abroad if we do our best to conform to local custom and practice but at the same time allow the brilliance of our ideas to show through. Avoiding culture clash is the objective. If you were selling a manufacturing process in Scandinavia for example you would have to acknowledge their strong environmental concerns. If cross-cultural training is offered and you have a family make sure they are involved. Women and children can put their foot in it too.

Take a small gift
Something from Liberty's or Harrods with the store's name on the product or gift wrapping is appreciated the world over.

Avoid the gift of wine in wine-producing countries and all food, except for hand made chocolates purchased locally. A good malt whisky is a status symbol everywhere but not appreciated in Muslim countries. Consider a photographic essay of historic Britain or one of its major cities.

Women travellers

Women who travel abroad on business need to be specially careful that they don't send out the wrong messages that signify lack of authority or sexual availability. Avoid potential problems by making your professional status clear, dressing smartly but conservatively and by calling yourself 'Mrs'.

TOP TIP

It is a severely career-limiting move to take a one-person-education campaign to a country where you are a guest. If the customs of the host country are going to offend you that much – *Don't go!*

Way 66 When abroad – speak the language

Language skills are the skills of the future, particularly in sales and marketing where fluency could bring in extra business. Fluency will undoubtedly be rewarded by a substantial increase in salary if it impacts on the bottom line. If you don't speak the language at least take the trouble to learn the correct way to meet and greet clients in their own country. At the very least take the time and effort to learn to say *and to recognise when you hear* some basic social and business phrases. Most hosts will find this flattering and will not see it as ingratiating.

TOP TIP

Being asked to work abroad for the first time is both exhilarating and alarming. Veteran business travellers say above all build goodwill before you attempt to do business.

Way 67 Be an effective networker

It is said that being successful in business is all about who you know. If this is true, then you must develop the skills of networking. Making new business contacts in order to ask them for a job is a bit like prostitution. This is not effective networking, it's embarrassing.

The benefits

- Discovering the hot issues in other industries, professions and parts of the country.
- The social element is attractive if you work anti-social hours or on your own.
- The chance of meeting someone who knows someone who can help you out.
- Building a network of professional and business acquaintances can be life-enhancing and a by-product could be a contract or a job of a lifetime.
- You can develop a reputation as a connector, bringing people together who can benefit from each other.

Beginner's guide to networking

Have a good supply of business cards with you at all times. Keep them handy. Exchange them with everyone you meet. They are a very inexpensive form of advertising. There's no point hanging on to them. When you receive someone else's card, make a note on the back of the date and the event where you met them and a personal note so that you can recall them if need be. If you meet a mutually interesting contact, make the call sooner rather than later, next day if possible before they forget you or the point.

Take the initiative. Join a group of three but not two – they may be in love. Introduce newcomers to your group and move on.

Perfect your 30–word statement (see Way 48) and trot it out smoothly and without hesitation. Have alternative presentations rehearsed and ready for different aspects of your business or interests. Have one presentation which closes with a goal or objective: ' . . . so after today's experience I am

looking for a conference centre with business TV facilities.'
' . . . so I am just about ready to think of moving back into
local politics.'

TOP TIP

When you are away on business, check whether there is
a branch of your network there. Ask if you would be
welcome to attend. If there is a guest list, study it to see
who you would like to meet and then aim to find them.
Introduce yourself and include a reason for wanting to
meet them.

Way 68 At a staff 'do': do the done thing when you are the guest

In most organisations people are recruited for their talent,
their technical know-how or specialist knowledge, not for
their social skills. Even so, a promising career can be wrecked
if you do not know how to behave in work-related social situations. Loners and disapprovers should at least turn up and
make an effort to join in. The situation needs a generous
helping of good humour, tact and diplomacy. The combination of flirting, free drinks and power games is a potentially
lethal cocktail for any career.

What to wear
Deciding what to wear can be tricky. Formal occasions requir-
ing white tie or black tie have their own set of rules and con-
sequently are easier to dress for because both men and
women can hire everything they need. Many organisations
will have built up traditions of partying over the years. If you
can't decide what to wear – ask. Get an opinion from someone senior as well as one of your peers. If in doubt, choose
something conservative. Your sparkling personality can make
up for it. Something too glamorous or quirky is impossible to
cover with witty conversation.

Because you are technically still at work, unless you have

been specifically asked to dress down or dress up, the usual rules of business dress apply but with a party feel. Women should avoid anything that is too short, too tight or exposes too much flesh. Men may remove their ties and jackets if things hot up a bit – but not their shirts or trousers.

If it's not the sort of occasion where everyone dresses up, then the aim is to look as though you've made some effort without appearing over-dressed. A smarter jacket, clean shirt, fresh shave for men; some jewellery, fresh make-up, change of top or jacket for women. Bring the items in with you and change at work.

Increasing your visibility
Use the occasion to introduce yourself as an individual, not just someone who occupies an office or fulfils a function. Buttonhole a superior but don't use the meeting to whinge.

When to arrive
Arriving a little early might mean a chance to talk to the hosts. If that misfires and no one else has turned up, an offer to help with drinks, table plans or other party arrangements can win you friends. Arriving very late needs an apology and a good excuse.

When to leave
Leaving conspicuously early needs an apology and a short believable explanation. Make an effort to find the host to say thank you and goodbye.

TOP TIP

If you make a fool of yourself – apologise. Make it short, private and face-to-face if possible or a note marked 'Confidential' if not. All that's required is: 'I'm sorry about what happened last night and I would like to apologise.'

Way 69 Organise the perfect party

If you are the host the occasion should be fun for you and your guests. You will want people to remember a good time and think of you as a considerate and generous host. Put some effort into the planning or delegate it to someone who is a good organiser. There are some important decisions to be made that will help the event to go well:

- **The kind of event.** Decide whether it should be an informal supper, proper sit-down meal, dinner and dancing or buffet-style reception. If you don't want to exclude families then a barbecue has the advantage of informality, children can be invited and it doesn't matter if it's all a bit chaotic. There are fewer social minefields for the less confident members of the firm.

- **The venue.** Hotels and restaurants have all the experience so leave it to them. Otherwise the 'do' could be held in-house if the environment is pleasant enough. The drawbacks to holding an internal event are the need to rely on volunteers for some aspects, the disruption to routine on the day and the mess the day after.

- **Timing.** If local or on-site, start half an hour after the usual close of business. It should last for two hours only.

- **Invitation list.** Decide who to invite and how to invite them. Make it clear whether or not a guest or spouse is included in the invitation. Include some fresh faces from outside for added interest.

- **The menu.** If the event is basically drinks, small, tasty bits of food including a vegetarian selection served at regular intervals prevents people drinking on an empty stomach. Nuts and crisps won't do.

- **Smoking.** It's mean not to let the smokers have a cigarette, particularly if there is a no-smoking policy at work.

- **Drink.** Be generous but offer a limited choice. Chilled white wine or good quality red plus mineral water and some interesting soft drinks served in nice glasses are normally sufficient. People can't expect you to provide a full bar. Serious beer drinkers can always reconvene at the pub later.

93

- **Transport.** It is thoughtful to provide transport to and from the venue if it is out of town, a long way from your usual place of work, or the weather is particularly baleful.
- **Accommodation.** Offer overnight accommodation if you anticipate a late finish, or to intercept guests who might drink and drive.
- **Your role.** Be there at the door to welcome everyone, use open and approachable body language, circulate, pull up a chair at different tables, join different groups, don't monopolise any individuals or groups.

TOP TIP

Leave early!

Way 70 Be an ambassador for your organisation at social events

Whatever the event, you are still at work and are very much a representative of your organisation. You are on duty and so you need to dress appropriately, behave properly, and not drink too much, however tempting. At a large social gathering such as a retirement party or at a 'free ticket' event like Ascot or Covent Garden there will be business friends and acquaintances and many individuals who are strangers to you. In the circumstances it is as well to make a favourable impression. At a wedding, for example, if they don't already know you, introduce yourself to the bride and groom and their families, explain who you are, why you are there and who you are representing. Give the present and make sure you convey the appropriate greetings. They will remember and appreciate the gesture long after they forget who you are. This is one of the few occasions when a thank-you note could be on the firm's letterhead.

If you feel uncomfortable at this kind of event but duty dictates that you should go, it might be helpful to spend some time on a bit of PMA – positive mental attitude. Enjoy the atmosphere and the surroundings, indulge in a little harmless people-watching and entertain your friends and family with your observations afterwards. Prime yourself for the event by being open and receptive in your mind, approachable in body language, correctly dressed and with some small talk. Comfort yourself with the thought that it can't last forever and that your presence is working towards polishing your image for the future. You can't sustain this for too long so do the right thing, leave as early as is polite to do so. Be happy in the knowledge that your professional image is still intact.

TOP TIP

A hand-written note following a big social 'do' is charming because it takes time and requires a little more effort.

Way 71 Be prepared to attend in-house ceremonies

Some organisations make quite a fuss of the life-changing events of their employees. Leaving the firm because you are moving abroad, retiring, having a baby or getting married are marked with a party and a present. A promotion, a hard-won new client or case solved are cause for a mini-ceremony.

If you can make a speech or present a gift at one of these occasions without looking awkward or being pompous you will add even more sparkle to the gloss of your image. Volunteer anyway and make sure someone takes your photo with the star.

TOP TIP

When making a speech at an internal ceremony, take it seriously but keep it light. Make it personal, sincere and very short.

Business-to-business communication

Way 72 The telephone: know the techniques

Body language and facial expression provide clues that smooth the course of face-to-face communication. We have to operate without these visual cues when using the phone and have to rely solely on the words we use and the silences in between. You must manage the impact of your telephone manner in the same way that you would manage your visual impression. Vocabulary, pitch and tone carry the message and act as cues to help us identify the attitudes and emotions behind the words.

Some useful techniques
- If you smile when you speak it makes the tone more pleasant. Look at yourself in a mirror when you are talking on the phone; watch for sullen expression or lack of animation.
- Stand up when you want to sell an idea, to be more assertive or more enthusiastic.
- Make a list of the main points before you call. Have the file open on the computer or the paperwork to hand.
- Make it a rule to return incoming calls within 24 hours.
- Try to answer on the first or second ring.
- Avoid taking calls when you have someone with you.
- Avoid talking to someone in the room while you are making a call.
- Avoid ending calls with a babyish 'By-ee' or a silly catch phrase unless you know the caller very well and they share the same sense of humour.
- Don't try to memorise important phone numbers, however good you think your memory is. One day you will mix them up for sure.

- Always call for a reason not just a chat.
- Making a good impression means making the other person's name the last word they hear.

Dedicated lines

If you run your own business from a home base or work for your organisation from home you must have a dedicated line. It keeps the finances separate, it gives a more professional impression and there is less intrusion from one area of life to the other. Teach your family to answer the phone clearly and politely and reduce background noises.

TOP TIP

If you can't reach someone important in another organisation because they are constantly unavailable or you can't get past their gatekeeper, obtain the number of their direct line, try calling before eight o'clock or after six. People at the top often work longer hours than any one else.

Way 73 Be an effective telephone listener

Not many of us have been taught to be effective listeners. We hear, so we think we listen. Nowhere are good listening skills more important than on the phone. Your professional image can be damaged by jumping to conclusions or not getting all the facts. Three levels of listening have been identified by specialists working for British Telecom:

- **Level 1**

  Known as active listening. The listener remains objective throughout the entire length of the conversation. The listener attempts to understand the other person's viewpoint and pays attention to the underlying pattern of what is being said as well as to the words themselves.

- **Level 2**

  Listening only to the 'surface' of the communication. Trying to hear what the speaker is saying but making no effort at understanding his or her intent. Characterised by being emotionally detached from the conversation and not participating in the interaction.

- **Level 3**

  Characterised by listening only in spurts, tuning in and out, and following a conversation only long enough to chip in the odd word. Possibly faking attention and remaining passive.

TOP TIP

If you find yourself on the receiving end of verbal abuse, don't take it personally. Stay calm, remain loyal to your company and let the caller talk themselves out.

Way 74 Recognise the barriers to effective listening

It's useful to learn to recognise the barriers that prevent the real message from being heard.

Emotional barriers

Maybe there are memories of the last time you spoke when you were upset, stressed or tired. If you dislike the caller's accent or they are not very articulate you may not give their ideas much consideration.

Physical distractions

Doing more than one thing at a time and spreading your attention, or trying to communicate above noise and activity means you are listening at level 3 and will not hear clearly all that is said (see Way 73).

TOP TIP

Prejudice can make you deaf.

Way 75 Use the answerphone as a butler

We don't have to answer the phone. Just because it's ringing doesn't mean it's urgent. Keep your answerphone on if you are trying to work or you have a meeting. It can screen your calls and act as a butler or secretary announcing that you are not at home but a message can be left. Group return calls for a more convenient time.

Leaving a message
Keep it short and to the point, don't hog finite tape space. Don't leave messages of a private or confidential nature, they may cause upset, offence or embarrassment in a shared office. Many machines can record day, date and time of call, but leave them anyway plus your name and call-back number. Add your surname if you have a common first name.

Taping a recorded announcement
The message should be assertive but not too bright or amusing. It should just confirm that the caller has hit target. Requests to speak clearly and leave your name and state the nature of your business are irritating and only consume units on the caller's telephone bill.

Inside story
Once when I was away on business, I settled down in my hotel room to catch up on the day's business via the remote access facility of the answerphone. One call was from a brusque chap who said he wouldn't leave a message as he didn't do business with answerphones. A bit of detective work found me the company number and I called the next day. I had definitely lost the business but won another important piece of information: I learnt that the man's business style matched his telephone style. Rude, impatient and peremptory – I wouldn't have wanted to work with him anyway.

> ### TOP TIP
> Return calls within 24 hours.

Way 76 Transmit facts faster: fax your message

Fax is fast. It enables same-day decisions. Faxing proposals to clients at midnight could misfire. Many people come in first thing and throw it all away, thinking it's unsolicited advertising.

It's as well to make the difference between business and social usage. Never fax a thank-you note. Fax directions but not an invitation. Being faxed an invitation to a business or social event is like being invited as an afterthought.

> ### TOP TIP
> Top and tail a social fax in your own handwriting.

Way 77 Use the mobile: choose your moment

The mobile phone is another one of those master strokes of technology that make us wonder how we ever managed without it. They have their disadvantages in terms of professional impact. Drusilla Beyfus, author of *Modern Manners,* is of the opinion that mobile phones can '. . . convey the impression that the user is indifferent to those around them, the definition of bad manners'.

> ### TOP TIP
> Never use a mobile phone in church, the Savoy or at Wimbledon.

Way 78 Make the right connections: join the Internet

There are thousands if not millions of software companies, service providers and Internet enthusiasts who would be only too pleased to help you take your first steps on the Information Highway. This world-wide resource can be of enormous benefit in your business life. You can use the Web to trawl through endless databases of information on business topics as well as entertain yourself by joining discussion groups on anything from anthropology to ethical marketing.

A PC 486 and above, a modem and a service provider will get you started. In its simplest form, an electronic mail system which can send messages down a phone line can be used to retrieve information from a variety of sources and can also be used as a messaging system for colleagues and clients. Used sparingly and carefully it is an efficient way to inform a select group of people about your news or update them on the latest developments.

'The aliens will think there is intelligent life on earth.'

Microsoft Windows '95 advertising campaign

TOP TIP

E-mail is an excellent way to provide up-to-date information in brief about what's going on. No explanations are needed, just the news

---

Way 79 Use your business card as a symbol of rank and recognition

You can't do business without a business card. A business card is not just an aid to identification and a means of introduction, it is also a symbol of rank and a means of recognition that can be used within the organisation or the wider business community. It should be in keeping with your status, be printed on good quality card in a regular size and format or else it will be thrown away because it won't fit any of the standard storage systems.

A charming business card and utterly to the point was one from a reflexologist. It was designed simply in black on white with her name, address of consulting rooms, paging service number, and a small footprint on the left hand corner.

If your company are mean about issuing business cards arrange to have your own simple design printed with your name, designation and contact details. It is bad form to try and reproduce your company logo. 'Stickies' will not do in a business context.

TOP TIP

If you staple your card to some information you are sending out, staple it face down and write a short message on the back. The card is asking to be turned over and your name will be triggered every time the piece is referred to.

Way 80 Project quality: your CV is an example of your work

Curriculum Vitae – from the Latin 'course of life' – a brief account of one's education, qualifications and previous occupations. It is actually your sales brochure not your life history.

Your CV needs to create the right impression from the start. There are fashions in CVs just as there are fashions in skirt lengths or management theory. You can put it on video or present it to a computer to be scanned for key words. Most importantly your CV is a marketing document and should be hand tailored for each post, kept up to date and beautifully presented. It should say who you are, how you can be reached and what you've been doing; which industry sector you've been in, your experience as a generalist or specialist, broadly or narrowly based, and in a lead or support role.

Style
- Scrap the cover page. Use good quality paper, white or off-white, textured but not coloured, lots of white space, clear and logical typography.
- Number and code each page with your name and date.
- Double check for spelling mistakes and 'typos'.

- Don't include a photo unless asked to. If you need one, get it done professionally.
- Don't bind or staple the CV.
- Do your own CV. If you are skilled at word processing, this means that you can tailor your CV for each post easily and elegantly without a secretary or agency.

TOP TIP

If you want to use a specialist CV agency make sure the accompanying documentation is in the same style, on the same paper and to the same standard as the CV that they produce for you. Otherwise it's a dead give away.

Way 81 Use your CV as an effective marketing tool

An easily scanned, professional-looking document which is your sales brochure should be no more than three pages long. If the CV looks good then the interviewer has every right to expect that you will too.

Experts don't always agree. The following notes have been built from the best of what the experts have to say. A welcome CV would look something like this:

1. Structure

Page 1	*Page 2*	*Page 3*
Personal data	Career summary	Interests
Short personal profile	Track record	Referees
Education	Achievements	Salary range
Qualifications		Personal
Present post		

2. Personal data

- Name and telephone number in bold or large type.
- List all telephone numbers, home, work, direct line, fax. Make it easy for anyone to contact you.
- Include date of birth and age even if you are sensitive about it.

- Put the bad news at the end if you think your age, or lack of appropriate background or experience could disad vantage you.

3. Short personal profile

- Your byline in about 30 words. (Some selectors like to see this, others find it meaningless.)

4. Education

- Show your education in reverse chronological order.
- State GCSE, O and A level subjects gained, include non-academic subjects (some selectors like to see the breadth of your background).
- State where you went to school, college, university.

5. Qualifications

- Start with those gained most recently. Include study in progress and expected pass date.
- State where you obtained your qualifications, with dates and special results.

6. Present post

- A succinct description of your role, responsibilities, bud get, staffing, sites.
- Try to match current assets, skills and achievements to those required on the job description.
- Talk up previous posts if they give you extra credibility or fill an achievement gap.

7. Career summary

- Try ordering in three columns: (1) the job, (2) the organi-sation, (3) the dates.
- Put in reverse chronological order and include less detail the further back it goes.
- Be prepared to explain any gaps or any peculiar sound ing job titles.
- Be accurate and truthful. Most things can be checked via the Internet.
- If you have been made redundant, say so.
- If you have been in the same job for five to ten years, break it down into elements.

8. Track record, list of achievements

- Structure under the same headings as the job description, person specification or key words in the advert.
- Rank your responsibilities.
- Sell the benefits.
- Use the organisation's language style and vocabulary.

9. Referees

- Don't put them on your CV or application form unless specifically asked to, wait until asked. 'References avail able on request' is enough.
- Referees should be more senior than you with high visibility or a credible professional title.
- Approach them first, tell them which aspects of your skills and personal qualities you would like them to high light.

10. Salary

- Private sector, don't include it. Public sector, most posts are graded and the application will probably ask for your present grade.

11. Interests

- Speaking another language or learning one as a social skill will become more and more of a business asset in the future.
- Membership of committees should indicate your role and special interest.
- Be prepared to talk enthusiastically and knowledgeably about your interests.

12. Personal

- Marital status, children, driving licence etc. Put at the end, in brief. We all have personal and private lives which are part of our total selves. No need to hide it. Be comfortable with your support systems and lifestyle but don't oversell them.

TOP TIP

'A welcome CV is one with a sense of the person behind it, one that shows me they have put some real thought into writing it, telling me what they have achieved and how they've got there. Misdirected gimmicks go straight in the bin.'

Debbie Walker, graduate human resource manager

Way 82 Write a strong covering letter

If recent letters of application have failed to hit the spot you may wonder why. The personnel manager or the graduate recruitment organiser is on the receiving end of thousands of applications for jobs. The current ratio is 100 applications for each job. When the forms come in they are sorted into three piles: (1) 'Yes, worth another look', (2) 'Maybe' and (3) 'In the bin'. This last pile fills up quickly with letters that:

- have no signature;
- are illegible;
- have applied for the wrong post or to the wrong company;
- say things like 'I'm a kinda wild and wacky sorta guy';
- are carefully pencilled and then inked over the top.

The 'yes' pile will be easy to read, laid out in several paragraphs and on no more than one page. They will contain a good sales pitch, emphasising what you can do for the organisation as well as what you want out of the job, how your skills, qualities and achievements match those of the job specification and give the reader a flavour of your personality and strengths. Jim Parton in *The Bucks Stop Here*, an autobiographical account of a bone idle, under-motivated stockbroker in the City, claims that there are 'strong strengths' and 'weak strengths'. Weak strengths include:

- I like people (= wimpy liberal)
- I am honest (= naive)
- I am a nice chap (= naive wimpy liberal)
- I work hard (everyone says that, unlikely to be believed)

Most recruiters would like to read evidence of what they can't advertise for and find it impossible to interview for. Parton's suggestions include:

- a cast-iron client base;
- instinctive, unforced clubability;
- being street wise;
- being 'hungry', having a driving ambition born of insecurity.

TOP TIP

Don't use attention-grabbing gimmicks, they've all been tried before.

Way 83 Application forms

We might loathe application forms but the company sending them out will have spent time and effort designing them and have a system for processing them. High-handedness, carelessness or coffee stains will make sure it lands up in the bin. Fill in the forms exactly as requested. If you don't show the company you are willing to play the corporate game at this early stage – forget it.

TOP TIP

Have several attempts at answering the questions in rough before committing your answers to paper. Check whether answers need to be typed or handwritten. Borrow a portable typewriter for the finished product if necessary and take a photocopy before you post it.

Way 84 Write a report that gets read

Impenetrable prose does not impress. An elegant, clear style will support your professional image. A well-written report will demonstrate logic and a clear flow of ideas. Accuracy is also important, so buy your own reference books if they are not readily available. Whatever your own style, take into account the house style of your organisation or the target organisation. There are four clear stages:

1. Preparation

2. Writing the material

3. Presentation and design

4. Checking

If you are not used to writing and presenting reports this is a default plan:

Title page
Contents
Summary – put it at the beginning but write it last.
Introduction – state your case using meaningful and logical headings and sub-headings
Conclusions
Recommendations – clearly stated in action terms
Appendices
Bibliography – if needed
References – if needed; if not clear from the main report
Index – key words can help the person who does not want to read the whole report
Glossary/Abbreviations – if many unfamiliar or technical words are used. It might be kinder to the reader to explain them in the text

---

TOP TIP

The finished result should be beautifully presented in a simple binder.

Way 85 Get into print

If you've never been published, what's stopping you? Five common reasons why people prevent themselves from getting into print are:

1. Miss Perfect. Yes, of course your piece will need some tweaking but getting it absolutely right is a familiar delaying activity.
2. Mr Ideas Man. Rid yourself of the notion that getting ideas is more important than writing about them. Ideas only have life when they are shared with others. Incomplete and over-researched books fill filing cabinets the world over.
3. 'Someone could steal my idea.' Be generous, share your thoughts, encourage debate. No one could do it like you could do it anyway.
4. 'I'm too busy.' Find more time by dumping what you don't like doing.
5. Inertia.

What are the benefits to being published?
- **Communication**. If you work on your own or in a specialist field, being published gets you a wider audience and opens up opportunities for debate and discussion with other experts, particularly with opportunities for joining in a debate via the Internet.

- **Credibility**. A published article undoubtedly lends credibility to your ideas.

- **Creativity**. Writing for your own pleasure, even in the form of a daily diary or a holiday journal can be enjoyed as a counterpoint to your usual daily duties and a pleasure in its own right.

- **Recognition**. An article in a trade journal that is widely read will gain you professional recognition.

- **Reward**. Writing articles can provide you with an income. If getting paid to write is important to you, you must first source the journals and magazines that use freelance writers and will pay for their work.

How do you go about getting published?
Match the product to the market. Talk to the editor or publisher about your idea.

Pay attention to packaging and presentation. Make it a pleasure to read. Double spaced throughout, 4cm margins right and left make it easier for an editor or reviewer to read and make comments. Print on good quality plain white paper. Send the required number of copies. Check that you have put a page number and identification on each page. Check for spelling errors, 'typos', proper names, capitalisation, technical terms. Organise yourself and your material so that you come across as being professional.

TOP TIP

Keep an ideas file. Keep cuttings, clippings, photos, cartoons and so in an expanding file. Open a file in your word processor to store your ideas. Whatever you are involved in at the moment could be turned into the makings of an article.

Way 86 Be a proficient pen-pusher: develop your writing skills

Writing is a real chore for so many of us. We drag the memory of school essays and exams with us into business life and this hampers our ability to put things down on paper when necessary. We either end up being pompous or producing waffle. Many professionals need to write clearly and concisely: the legal secretary, the occupational therapist, the social worker all have to write to clients and write up reports; the site manager will have to write to suppliers and solo consultants must write proposals and recommendations to their clients.

Spelling and grammar
Does it matter if you can't spell? Is an insistence on correct spelling just another authoritarian conspiracy or an example of cultural imperialism? The fact is that grammatical and

spelling mistakes put the message out of focus for a literate reader.

These simple guide-lines should go some way to repairing the legacy of a State education system that put literacy last.

1. As a first step consider who is likely to be your reader and what do they want to know.

2. Think, plan, then write.

3. Make it interesting by using illustrations from as wide a territory as you can. From fell-walking to fanzines, from *haute couture* to hagiology.

4. Write as you speak then edit it.

5. Try for a balance between long and short words, long and short sentences, simple ideas and more complex ones.

6. If grammar is not your strength, read your piece aloud, your voice will drop at natural punctuation points.

7. Run it through the Fog Index,* or style check programme on your PC to see how easy it is to understand.

This is an example from a letter to my company:

'It would be appreciated if you could inform me whether your company would be able to facilitate this kind of requirement, and if you could additionally provide me with some general information on the services that your organisation can offer.'

I translated that to mean:

'Please send me information about your company and its services.'

---

* Robert Gunning's Fog Index – a system of calculating how many years' formal education is required to understand a piece of writing. The Fog index rating of the passage you have just read (Way 86) is 16, and should be understood by graduates.

'To refuse to obey the rules [of spelling] is not to win your freedom but simply to drop out of the game. The mistake is to think that a spelling rule is like a repressive moral law when actually it is a guide to intelligibility.'

Janet Daley, journalist and broadcaster

TOP TIP

Increase your word power. Use a Thesaurus to look up alternative words, make sure you read regularly, look up the meaning of words you don't know, do crossword puzzles.

Way 87 Keep a career portfolio

Compile a portfolio of all your achievements that have been documented. Attendance certificates, qualifications, commendations, references, reports, brochures – include anything you have designed or had a significant part in such as course design, course materials, training programme, induction event. Look for a presentation folder with transparent pockets. If an item is too large for the folder replace it with a card that states where it is stored. If it is very small attach it to a piece of card that fits the pocket. If you are not a natural archive keeper then put a note in your diary to keep it topped up and organised every couple of months or so.

There are two benefits to this exercise:

1. You will have everything to hand to take to or help you plan for an interview.
2. You can remind yourself how much you've achieved.

TOP TIP

Arrange your career portfolio in reverse chronological order. Start at the back so that your most recent achievements are at the front.

Way 88 Keep a cuttings and clippings file

This is your personal or organisation's PR record. Keep anything that has your name on it in a presentation folder, scrap
book, box file or album. You might find it interesting to look
back on and remind yourself about good ideas and effective
past publicity. A press cuttings agency will trawl the press for
you for a fee.

TOP TIP

Newspaper cuttings can be preserved better if they are
clipped to stiff paper and stored in transparent wallets.
The paper can be marked up with the date and name of
the journal if it is missing.

Way 89 Keep in the frame with a good photo

Have a set of professional black and white photographs
taken. Don't rely on the passport photo booths. They always
make you look vaguely criminal when reproduced. Use the
photos for internal and external PR, for conference pro-
grammes when you are invited to speak and to accompany
articles for professional journals. Colour photos and action
shots are more likely to be used than a black and white head
and shoulders portrait.

TOP TIP

Good quality copies are available cheaply from repro-
graphics shops. There are several good and reliable
firms who advertise in *The Stage* every week.

Way 90 Keep a victory log

This is an on-going log of all your successes and achievements. This idea has similar objectives to Way 87. Keep a

career portfolio; the difference is that this log contains the victories, large and small, that might not get an honourable mention in any other way. Things like being polite to a particularly obnoxious customer, conquering your nerves and doing a good presentation, coming out of a tricky negotiation with dignity, persuading someone to change their mind, saving time with a new system, mastering a new technique and so on.

TOP TIP

When your self-esteem is a little low, bring out the 'Victory Log' and allow it to drop open at random like the pages of *I Ching* and let its contents warm and surprise you.

Way 91 Use your design portfolio as your passport to see people

If you design, draw, paint or sculpt be as loving and extravagant as you can with the presentation of your portfolio. It is the overture to your means of earning your living. It represents you when you are not there. It is your sales brochure.

- Never leave your portfolio with anyone other than your agent. Your work could get lost, stolen, damaged or ripped off, as I know from bitter experience when I was a raw young designer eager for work in the rag trade.
- The portfolio itself should be of good quality and robust enough to stand being hauled round the country.
- Your name and address and telephone number and details of your agent should appear on every single item as well as the portfolio itself.
- If you use colour slides to illustrate large or three-dimensional work label them clearly with their title and your address etc. Always carry a slide viewer.

TOP TIP

Include a brief biography with a list of published work, exhibitions, patrons, awards and commissions at the front or back. Well presented and easy to read, it looks impressive and business-like. Like a CV it should contain the best and most recent work at the top.

Way 92 Save backs of envelopes: the best ideas need a business plan

A world-beating idea on the back of an envelope will be recognised for what it is, regardless of the presentation. To keep our professional image secure we must present our business ideas as crisply and persuasively as possible. This doesn't just apply to a business plan that the bank manager will appraise before you start up in business but also to business ideas presented internally or externally.

A business plan should obey all the rules of good written business presentation (see Ways 84 and 86) and have two special added ingredients:

1. The sums must add up; and
2. Someone must want to buy it.

TOP TIP

'What I look for in an entrepreneur is an attitude of: There will be no excuses from me. In other words an internal locus of control.'

Jamsheed Engineer, MD, The Transcultural Consultancy

Press, People and Politics

Way 93 Check for sound: using radio

Radio is an excellent medium if you enjoy a debate and thinking on your feet. Most of my experience has been with local radio. One thing I learnt early on was that the listeners do not make allowances for an amateur. They are inclined to take the side of the presenter who is the familiar voice and presence. Getting ratty or over-emotional might make interesting radio for a few moments but spoils your reputation for a lot longer. Don't call the interviewer by name – they are not your audience, the listeners are: your sound-bite might be needed on another programme.

Live recording
It may be scary but a live contribution can't be cut or used out of context. Take a cassette tape with you and ask someone to record the interview for you. If you find yourself in a self-operating studio then there will usually be a self-recording facility in the studio. Ask a technician to help you with this when you arrive. The BBC have clear instructions pinned on the wall telling people how to manage their own interview, including instructions about how to record their own tape to take away.

Get there a little early. There are not many spare staff on a small radio station and they have to perform many tasks at once, so be prepared to be ignored. Try to build some kind of rapport with the presenter before the interview begins. At least make eye contact. The presenter will be concentrating on the technicalities of keeping the show moving, keeping to time, playing the jingles, fitting in the news reports and so on, as well as and getting a contribution out of you.

Relax the voice

A popular technique is to breathe in then on the out breath say – A E I O U – very slowly, stretching and working the mouth. Say it several times, pitching it higher and lower by turn then waggle your jaw from side to side just before you speak.

Telephone link-up

The producer will ring you in advance to book you, then again a few minutes before the slot to make sure you are actually there and are willing and able to speak, and also to get a voice level.

Phone-in

Don't read your question or observation; you'll sound half-witted.

Panel guest

If your fellow guests are in another studio the rules of polite conversation do not apply. You can not pick up visual clues about when the other speaker has finished speaking so you may not know when it's your turn to speak. The presenter, if they are competent, will want to prevent everyone talking at once but ensure the air space is filled. Listen very carefully for the presenter to prefix a question with your name. This is your permission to speak.

Ask for a fee

Expenses or a fee are sometimes available. It's your time and professional expertise, so put a value on it. You might not get either but it's worth asking.

Sound advice

Listeners get distracted by unnecessary noise. Francis Pearce, a radio journalist who also trains company personnel in media techniques, lists distractions that could be picked up by the microphone:

- jangling jewellery;
- metallic buttons;
- banging the table;
- tapping your pen;
- rustling paper;
- loud watch;
- grabbing hold of the microphone;
- having the radio switched on;
- humming fridge or air conditioner;
- interruptions from cats, dogs, colleagues or family.

Inside story

CBC telephoned me in London from Toronto wanting my view on a controversial issue. They were worried about the sound quality and rang back several times to try to get a better line. They asked if there might be a problem with the hand set and was it a regular BT phone? Yes it was, so what could be the problem? When the interview was over I realised that because I was so tense I was grasping the receiver so tightly I made it creak.

TOP TIP

Don't swear. Don't get technical.

Way 94 Lights and camera: using TV, video and video-conferencing

TV studios can be hot and uncomfortable places. In these conditions it's all too easy to look ill at ease and less than professional. Those in the business would say that the camera makes no allowances for beginners' nerves or ignorance of the medium. Arm yourself in any way you can so that you do not get caught in the lights like an unwilling understudy at a rehearsal.

Stay camera sharp

Keep colours camera-sharp, medium tones of navy, grey, blues and greens always work. Avoid reds, black with white, and fine pin stripes, which have a tendency to strobe. When sitting down, sit well back in the chair, pull your jacket down at the back and sit on it. This prevents the jacket from rucking round the neck and shoulder area. Wear a distinctive tie that is timeless rather than screamingly up to date. Some tie designs can date you accurately to within a few months. If you are in the studio, take some alternative garments with you. Not only will they feel fresher and cooler but you can choose something that will come across well.

On video

A video recorder is often used on training courses to record presentations or role play. Video is a wonderful and immediate learning medium but you don't want your mistakes shown around. Enquire about confidentiality. Take the tape with you or obtain a guarantee that it will be wiped before re-use.

Video-conferencing

Video-conferencing removes the need for face-to-face contact. But it does not remove the need for powerful personal presentation and a strong, clear message. No amount of technological wizardry is going to compensate for a poor message. Video-conferencing and business television are not yet commonplace but more and more hotels and conference centres are investing in 'tomorrow's workplace' where people can meet each other via a satellite link-up.

TOP TIP

'Either the camera loves you or it doesn't. If you are offered help with make-up or hair accept it, this is not vanity it's just being professional.'

Alan Felton, actor and theatrical historian

Way 95 Understand the press agenda

Some things are guaranteed to get you into trouble. Positive Images Media have a well-tried list of DOs and DON'Ts when dealing with print media:

Do	*Don't*
Respond quickly.	Don't say anything that you
Ask what the story is for.	wouldn't want to read or
Know your message.	Don't panic.
List key points.	hear.
Put comments in context.	Don't try to be the editor.
Be honest and accurate.	Don't knock the opposition.
Prepare for tricky questions.	Don't assume they only
Specify 'off the record'.	want bad news.
Use embargoes sparingly.	Don't over-react to bad or
	no press.
	Don't expect to be quoted on
	your own.
	Don't link editorial and
	advertising.
	Don't offer a bribe.

TOP TIP

When preparing a story for the press, ask yourself 'So what?' – is it really news? Don't try to get a non-story into print.

Way 96 Make friends with the local press

Making your mark with the print media can be as important as getting your message across in the board room. Getting good coverage in the local or trade media not only helps sales but can also make recruitment easier. A good story in the local paper or a piece on the radio involving members of staff and the community can do wonders for marketing and morale.

> **TOP TIP**
> Develop a relationship not a reaction.

Way 97 Die-stamp your mark as a professional

Wally Olins has created a successful identity programme for the world's best known companies. He believes that: 'In today's fast changing business environment, a company must express its identity in everything that it does.' I believe that today's professional should follow the same path. From a formal business presentation to the state of the inside of their car to their fashion accessories, the impression they create should be die-stamped with the mark of a professional.

The same standards of professional presentation apply to the places you go to for lunch, your membership of clubs and associations, where you entertain clients and so on. There's no need to be a snob or even a reverse snob about it, but be aware of the messages that are attached to being seen in certain places.

The way you arrange your office or work station is not just your business. Your taste is on public display so don't think it won't be judged.

Look at your organisation and its image in terms of the parts that make up the whole:the reception area, the style of decor, furniture, fixtures and fittings in the building, the building itself, its location, its style of architecture and state of repair, the fleet of vans; visible and invisible personnel – reception, security, maintenance, switchboard, visiting consultants and directors.

You have chosen to work at this place. What does that say about you?

> **TOP TIP**
> Create your own professional identity programme and make sure everything you do is consistent with it.

Way 98 Become a politician

One of the prime reasons why otherwise bright individuals do not get the promotion they deserve is that they have failed to understand the significance of internal politics and have not built an intelligence network. They are not prepared to lean against the photocopier and exchange gossip with their colleagues about what is going on. For political success you need a power-base built on specialist knowledge, connections, or information.

Office politics do exist whether you work on a building site, a hospital ward or a board room. Wherever you work there will be internal politics. Everyone on the payroll from top to bottom and side to side is involved in political power games of one kind or another. People who are not prepared to play the game simply become the pawns of those who do (see Top Tip in Way 1). If you want to join the successful people in an organisation check whether you share key characteristics; do you know how to get things done; can you identify the movers and shakers and most importantly are you prepared to avoid offending the sacred cows.

Being a successful office politician means being prepared to please your superiors but not alienating your peers. It also means looking like a winner and adopting the team strip of the successful players.

TOP TIP

Acknowledge that some people play dirty. Be prepared to defend yourself.

Way 99 Observe the rules of business etiquette

Good manners in business may go unremarked but bad manners are never forgotten. Business etiquette includes:

- returning a phone call within 24 hours;
- replying to a letter in 48 hours;
- not bullying;

- not harassing;
- not being aggressive;
- not stealing other people's ideas;
- not using alcohol or cigarettes unless invited;
- not chewing gum in public;
- keeping your business and personal life separate;
- keeping your word.

TOP TIP

Extend common courtesies to colleagues and visitors. Don't keep them waiting, offer them coffee, a chair, help them off with their coat. Enquire after their families and their health.

Way 100 Snap up the right training and support

In the last decade we have been moving slowly away from the idea of a successful career that goes up in graded steps, measured by job title and salary and moved towards a personal agenda of job satisfaction and success. In the future, we will all need to become more entrepreneurial and find out where the growing opportunities are, both where we work now and in the world of work in general.

Access key business projects
To show-case your talents and provide opportunities for personal and professional development you will have to develop a nose for key business projects and how to access and become part of them, because that's where the training and development resources will be going in the future.

Self-managed learning
Sign up to the self-managed learning culture and make yourself responsible for identifying ways to refurbish your skills,

upgrade your knowledge, find opportunities for re-training, and learn how manage new business relationships.

Flexing your business personality
It is worth considering the distinction between 'career' and 'job'. Raymond Williams in *Keywords* reminds us that, from the sixteenth century, 'career' was used in connection with the race-course and the gallop and by extension any rapid, uninterrupted activity. In contrast 'job' means a piece of work for hire or profit, 'jobbing – working on occasional or separate jobs in order to earn a living'. We could consider the future with these two definitions in mind. Undoubtedly we will have to flex the whole of our business personality – interpersonal, management, leadership, strategic, technical, social and intrapreneurial skills – to meet changing needs.

THE BUSINESS PERSONALITY
Interpersonal Strategic Technical
Social Leadership Intrapreneurial
skills

Flexing your business personality

TOP TIP
Find out how a mentor or coach could help you with your career plans.

Way 101 Make the best of rumour, sensation and scandal

Gossip is fun. We love to know how other people live their lives, it shows we are interested in events and humanity. It's the malicious or spiteful rumours that get out of control which cause trouble. If the worst happens, my colleagues in press offices up and down the country would say that in order to keep your professional image intact :

- Maintain a dignified silence.
- Don't talk to the press, even off the record.
- Take the phone off the hook.
- Don't retaliate.
- Be polite and meanwhile work away at positive PR.
- Avoid any public engagements for a while.
- Go and stay with a discreet friend for a while.
- If you can trust yourself to make a statement without resorting to temper or tears make one within 24 hours. Get legal help with the statement and if there is any chance of a photo call – be perfectly presented.
- If you can't guarantee composure a third party should issue a short, concise *final* statement.

and finally . . .

- If all that attention is everything you've ever dreamed of then get serious and employ a media relations expert to milk it for all it's worth.

Inside story

A couple of years ago my company was involved in a front page 'bash the NHS story' to do with training courses in professional presentation for NHS consultants and managers. The 'Lipstick Lessons on the NHS' story broke on a Sunday morning just as I was due to go away on business for two days. I'll never forget the consultant who turned up the following morning showing her support by wearing a ceramic brooch in the form of bright red lips. On my return, home and work answerphones were full to capacity with calls from

125

journalists, alternately rude, irate or pleading, wanting my side of the story. Legal and press office advice was to sit it out and stay silent. The story blew itself out in three days. No one loves a whistle blower.

TOP TIP

When the fuss has died down, the best possible professional impact is made by putting up the 'Business as usual' sign.

Last word
Someone once said that Alcohol, Adultery and Arrogance were the three things guaranteed to bring down the best.

Further Reading from Kogan Page

12 Steps to Self-Improvement, Michael Crisp, 1992

The 20% Factor: How to Achieve Immediate 20% Improvement in Your Life, Your Skills, Your Job, Graham Lancaster, 1993

Assert Yourself – And Do a Good Deal Better With Others, Robert Sharpe, 2nd edn, 1989

Be an Achiever: A Handbook to Get Things Done, Geoffrey Moss, 1991

Developing Self-Esteem, Connie D Palladino, 1990

Great Answers to Tough Interview Questions, Martin John Yate, 3rd edn, 1992

How to Think on Your Feet, Patrick Quinn, 1994

The Image Factor, Eleri Sampson, 1994

Individual Excellence: Improving Personal Effectiveness at Work, Ralph Lewis and Phil Lowe

Interviews Made Easy: How to Get the Psychological Advantage, Mark Parkinson, 1994

Eleri Sampson is the Managing Consultant of Positive Images. For information about public seminars, corporate training workshops and personal consultations on effective self-presentation please contact:

Positive Images
32 Hazelbourne Rd
London SW12 9NS

Phone: 0181 675 5806
Fax: 0181 673 9020